What'$
YOUR
Rate?

What'$
YOUR
Rate?

HOW TO BUY A HOME AND SECURE YOUR FINANCIAL FUTURE AT THE SAME TIME

MARK MAIOCCA

WITH CONTRIBUTING AUTHORS:
CHUCK SILVERSTON AND WILLIAM TATOSKY

Published by Advantage, Charleston, South Carolina.
Member of Advantage Media Group.

ADVANTAGE is a registered trademark and the Advantage colophon is a trademark of Advantage Media Group, Inc.

Printed in the United States of America.

ISBN: 978-159932-341-1
LCCN: 2012945218

This publication is designed to provide accurate and authoritative information in regard to the subject matter covered. It is sold with the understanding that the publisher is not engaged in rendering legal, accounting, or other professional services. If legal advice or other expert assistance is required, the services of a competent professional person should be sought.

Advantage Media Group is proud to be a part of the Tree Neutral® program. Tree Neutral offsets the number of trees consumed in the production and printing of this book by taking proactive steps such as planting trees in direct proportion to the number of trees used to print books. To learn more about Tree Neutral, please visit www.treeneutral.com. To learn more about Advantage's commitment to being a responsible steward of the environment, please visit www.advantagefamily.com/green

Advantage Media Group is a leading publisher of business, motivation, and self-help authors. Do you have a manuscript or book idea that you would like to have considered for publication? Please visit www.advantagefamily.com or call 1.866.775.1696

To my mom and dad, Dominic and Phyllis Maiocca.
If it were not for you, I would not have my family, my
family values, and the memories that I cherish so dearly.

Ten percent of all net proceeds from the sale of this book will benefit One Mission, to help find a cure for pediatric cancer and better the daily living for the patients and their families.

www.onemission.org

Contents

Introduction

Why am I so passionate about the subjects of preparation and personal finance?

The year was 1986. I was living in a beautiful home in Newton, Massachusetts, with my mom, my dad, and my sister. My mom and dad had a thriving business and a second home on Cape Cod. They were making plenty of money and they were on top of the world.

Then my dad was diagnosed with cancer. It was terminal. Six weeks later, he was gone. He did not have life insurance.

Over the next five to seven years, I watched my mother work to put my sister and me through college, but her income was not enough to cover it all. She eventually had to sell our home in Newton for less than full value, her share of the second home in Cape Cod, and then her business. Altogether she cleared over $1,000,000, but it all went to pay off the debt she had accumulated. Because we had no insurance, this unexpected event took all of our money.

Guess what my mom and dad did for a living? *They sold insurance.* They sold homeowner's insurance. Before my dad died, my mom was in the process of getting her life insurance license. She was studying for the exam. It was a classic case of the old saying, "the cobbler's children have no shoes."

Years later, I got into the mortgage business and started to see the opportunity to really make a difference in people's lives. Many times, buying a home is the first major financial move a person or a family makes. I realized another thing—my parents sat with the same mortgage originator for the purchase of their first and second homes, a construction loan, and two refinances. They did five loans with the same mortgage originator and they used to say such nice things about him. The mortgage originator should have recognized the opportunity to recommend that my parents talk to a financial advisor about their insurance protection, but he didn't.

It made me wonder how I would feel if I were their lender, and I had assumed that because they were in the insurance business, they were all set and had already taken care of their insurance protection? Did their mortgage originator think it wasn't his responsibility to advise them on their insurance and their finances because he was facilitating the mortgage loan?

It is our responsibility.

People need to get their financial team in place as soon as possible. As a mortgage originator, I have the opportunity to introduce my team right when people make what is usually their first major financial move. I have the opportunity to change lives. My parents worked so hard, but they didn't receive the proper advice at the time they needed it most and that made all the difference.

This is a story about how change can happen and what it might mean for you. You'll learn about a very special team of people called the Core 7, and how powerful it is to have this team working for you and your family. If you do not have a Core 7 team in place, you and your family are financially exposed. Don't worry—assembling your team does not have to be a complicated process. This book will show you a simple way to get your whole financial house in order during a process many people go through: the purchase of a first home.

HOW TO GET THE MOST OUT OF THIS BOOK

If you are a professional who functions as a member of a Core 7 team, notice the Core 7 process in action as you read through the book: the system of scripts used to assist in familiarizing your clients with the process, the time when introductions are made, the questions that are asked, the words that are used when answering questions, and the teamwork that occurs at every point in the process. Make a flowchart of the process for your business. Are you or your team members missing any important steps?

If you are an individual looking to get your finances in order, notice how each Core 7 team member is key to the overall financial plan, and how each person is valuable in a specific aspect of one's financial life. Notice how a financial team can work better together if they are all on the same page and shooting for the same goals with your best interests in mind.

Also, notice how the home buying process works. Buying a home is an ideal time to get your financial team in place. Pay close attention to how the system is ongoing; the relational team carries on in pursuit of constant clarity for your goals.

ASK YOURSELF THESE QUESTIONS

(If you answer "no" or "I don't know" to any of them, you need to read this book.)

1. Do I have an advisor for all aspects of my financial plan?
2. Do I have enough time to manage all aspects of my personal finances?
3. If I were to die or become disabled, would I be able to support my family and my lifestyle, and maintain my assets?
4. If I were sued, are my assets safe?

5. Am I maximizing my tax savings?

6. Do I have someone managing my mortgage so that I always maintain the best interest rate and mortgage structure the market has to offer?

7. Do I know the value of my real estate?

8. Do I have a clear investment plan for real estate?

9. Do I know the exact return I want on my investment real estate?

10. If I die while my children are underage, do I know who their guardian would be?

11. If I were to die, would my assets be distributed properly?

12. If I were incapacitated, do I know who would make decisions for me and my family?

13. If interest rates on my mortgage were to drop, do I have someone who will notify me before it's too late?

14. Can I retire comfortably?

15. Am I aware of nursing home costs?

16. If a key member of my business were to die or become disabled, do I know what effect that would have on my business?

17. Can I sell my business right now?

18. Will my daughter or son be able to take over my business if I want to retire?

19. Are my financial goals in line with my life and family goals?

20. Do I have peace of mind?

For the professional:

1. Do you have a partnership with all of the Core 7 professionals (Financial Advisor, Estate Planning Attorney, Real Estate Attorney, Accountant, Mortgage Originator, Home Owners Insurance Agent, and Real Estate Agent)?

2. Do you have a systematic way to work with all of your partners?

3. Are your clients fully covered in all aspects of their financial plan?

4. Are you receiving referrals from the other six members of the Core 7 team?

I wrote this book because I believe that good financial planning helps families to weather adversity and keeps families together. It gives you the freedom and the opportunity to do the things that matter most to you. I hope this book will inspire you to get your Core 7 team in place right away. Get your family covered financially and focus on what's important, such as creating great memories with the ones you love.

CHAPTER 1

The Sign

Tom Rogers felt rich. Driving home from work that day he thought the car had wings. Kim's voice from their phone call still rang happily in his ears, "I'm pregnant—*again*." Just when they had accepted that they would not have any more children after their two young sons, now this! It was almost too much. Tom had a beautiful wife he had loved since college, a rambunctious 6-year-old, Tommy Jr., and a free-spirited 4-year-old, Ben. He had a job he loved, with opportunities for advancement. He couldn't ask for more and now here was this unexpected blessing—a new life on the way.

He steered toward the off ramp and made his way home to their apartment complex. Already Tom's mind was fast-forwarding to Kim's third trimester and all of the things he had to do before then. He was glad they hadn't given away all of the baby gear. He knew the crib sat in pieces somewhere in their storage area in the basement. He thought he remembered seeing the changing table somewhere down there as well. He'd dig it out, dust it off, bring it upstairs to their apartment and put it...where?

Tom stopped at a red light as a frown began to form deep ridges across his forehead. They only had two bedrooms. He and Kim had given the larger one to the boys. There was just enough room for their twin beds and a dresser. Tom and Kim could barely walk around the queen-sized bed in their own room. Since no more furniture would fit in the room, they had to keep all of their clothes stuffed into the one tiny closet. Come to think of it, Tom was tired of wearing wrinkled shirts and of having laundry piled on the bed because they had no place to put it.

The toys were an issue all on their own. It was hard enough getting Tommy Jr. and Ben to clean up their trucks, trains, and action figures at the end of the day. They hated trying to fit them into one toy chest. What would happen when they had baby toys strewn across the floor once again?

Tom shook his head remembering when, in their last apartment, Tommy Jr. had tried to draw a mural on his bedroom wall with magic markers. The landlord had flipped out and made them pay to have the whole room repainted. They had come very close to a similar scenario with Ben, but Tom managed to grab the pencil from his chubby little fingers before he jabbed it into the drywall.

He could feel his own fingers beginning to sweat on the steering wheel. He took a deep breath but could still feel the anxiety building up within him. When he envisioned his family's future he saw a messy, stressful existence in which his children couldn't ask their friends over because the apartment was in a constant state of chaos. He saw Kim and himself arguing over stupid things such as leaving a teabag on the kitchen counter and the fact that their home wasn't a restful place. Was that what he wanted for his family?

That's when he saw it: a thick white post holding up a real estate sign with blue and red lettering. Tom thought it was odd at first because there was no house in view, but then he realized the house must be down the road. There was a "Dead End" sign posted across from the real estate sign. Tom had never gone down that street before, but the sign made him curious. "Let's see what's down there," he said to himself.

The road wasn't too long—maybe less than half a mile—and Tom quickly saw that the Dead End was a generous cul-de-sac. Three houses lined part of the circle but the fourth, the one that had another sign posted in front of it, was just up a short driveway. Tom pulled into the drive and got out to examine the cul-de-sac. "What a great place to learn how to ride a bike," he thought. Where he lived now, the only flat, paved surface was a busy parking lot. The boys never set foot on it without holding his or Kim's hand, and riding bikes there was totally out of the question.

But this house seemed to have plenty of room to play. In fact, it had its own swing set perched on the edge of the lawn where the side yard met a small wooded area. Tom went up the walk to the front door. The door handle was encased in a big gray plastic contraption that appeared to be a lock. Tom looked around and then, cupping his hands around his eyes, he peered through one of the door's sidelights.

Tom smiled. To his left, he could see into a large dining room with polished hardwood floors and a curvy black iron light fixture hanging over the spot where the dining table would go. To the right, he could see a room with bookshelves lining the walls. Maybe it was a home office? Tom laughed. What a concept! To think he'd have a place to get work done—*at home.* The center hall led to what looked like a bright kitchen. There were carpeted stairs that went up to a second floor where Tom was pretty sure there would be more than two bedrooms.

What if he were coming home to this house? Tom could see Tommy Jr. and Ben thumping down the stairs to greet him. Maybe Kim would be feeding the new baby in a high chair in the kitchen. He'd get a welcome home kiss and the boys would beg him to come out and throw the ball around before dinner. "Come on Dad!" He would drop his briefcase in his home office and run out into the yard with them.

Tom stood there and breathed in the smell of the grass. He'd probably toss balls to Tommy Jr. and Ben and think about how he needed to mow the lawn over the weekend. But that was okay. He could live with that. What mattered most was this beautiful picture of his family smiling, relaxed, and feeling loved and whole in this new space—in their home.

Tom could feel his anxiety melting away. They would buy a house. He and Kim had been saving for a long time. Surely they could afford to buy now? He got back in his car and drove home. He couldn't wait to tell Kim about what he was thinking.

As he pulled into his assigned spot at the apartment complex, Tom saw his new neighbor, John Randle, getting out of his car too. John had moved in down the hall from them just a few months ago. Tom thought he seemed to be someone he would like to have had as a grandparent: nice, thoughtful, and always ready with a smile or an extra hand to help with herding the kids down to the car. Today John was dressed in a dark blue polo shirt and a windbreaker. He looked as if he had just played a round of golf; his gray hair looked tousled from the wind and his cheeks glowed.

"Hello there," John called to Tom. "You look like a man happy to be home."

"Oh, I'm just filled with good things going on," Tom said. "We just found out Kim is pregnant."

"Wonderful!" John said, and Tom could tell his reaction was warm and heartfelt. He offered Tom his hand and gave him a vigorous shake.

"Yeah, we're pretty excited. I'm thinking it might be time for us to get a house. Three kids would be a pretty tight fit for a two-bedroom apartment."

"Well, I would miss you, but that is good thinking. Got a place in mind?"

"We might. I just saw a place now that I really like."

"Good luck with it. This is a big step. Let me know if you need any help."

"Okay, thanks, John."

Tom reached his door and searched for his keys. He was thinking it was really nice of John to offer his assistance, but how much help could he be? He was a renter too. If he ever did own property, it was probably a house he had bought thirty years ago and sold when his children grew up. What would he know about the way things were today?

As he opened the door, he heard Tommy Jr. in full voice, "Mommy! Ben kicked over my train track again. I was trying to build it to go under the bed and now he broke it apart."

"No I didn't! No I didn't!" Ben protested. "It was an accident! It's in the way! It's on the floor! I was just trying to get on my bed!"

"Come on guys, just stop it." Kim's voice overrode all. "We can fix it, Tommy Jr. Come on, Ben, you help too."

Tom walked in to find Kim on her knees with the boys in their bedroom piecing back together wooden bits of train track. He didn't try to go in because there was no room. Kim looked up and smiled at him, pushing a stray blonde lock of hair out of her eyes. She looked tired. Tom thought his wife was an angel, but he could sense her frustration at times like this when she had been home with the boys for a few hours and they had started getting on each other's nerves. He had no idea how she managed to survive on snow days when she and the boys were cooped up in the apartment all day. Yet Kim was the one who kept their household running, the one who packed lunches and did laundry and paid bills and planned play dates and attended parent-teacher conferences. Would having a real home make her life easier? If it could, she definitely deserved it.

That night, after they had put the boys to bed, Tom told Kim about the real estate sign and how it had led to his idea that they should try to buy a house.

"I saw that sign too," Kim said as her face lit up. Tom thought it was worth mentioning if only to see Kim get so excited. "I didn't go down the street, though. Do you think we could see pictures of it online?"

"Yeah, let's check the company's website."

Tom pulled his laptop out of his briefcase, set it up on the coffee table, and turned it on. In a few moments they were scrolling through a handful of photos of the cul-de-sac home. He had been right about the kitchen. It was bright and airy and was big enough for a breakfast table. There was also a built-in desk along one wall. "The kids could do their homework there while I cook dinner," Kim said. The upstairs had four bedrooms including a master with its own bathroom. "All of the kids could have their own rooms, even the baby," Tom said. "Can you imagine having so much space?"

"But can we afford it?" Kim frowned at the asking price and the estimated taxes. "I mean, this would be so wonderful, Tom, but can we really do it?"

"I don't know." Tom scrolled down to find the number of the realtor showing the house. "But I promise you, Kim, I'll figure it out. Let's go see the house. Seems to me like a good place to start."

CHAPTER 2

A Home of Our Own

"She looks pretty upbeat," Tom observed as he and Kim watched Ms. Gwendolyn Davis pull into the driveway in a large, silver luxury sedan. "Maybe she knows already that we really want this house. I told her we didn't need to see any other homes with her."

"Well, why should we look at a bunch of other houses?" Kim pulled a notebook out of her purse. "We don't even know if we can afford it yet and besides, this is the one we like."

Tommy Jr. and Ben had been running around in the yard for ten minutes and looked ready to make their first assault on the swing set. "Okay." Tom took a deep breath and looked at Kim. "Let's go."

Ms. Davis hopped out of her car and straightened her brown pencil skirt. She reached back in to retrieve a heavy, red, briefcase-type bag that she slung over her shoulder. "Ted! Kate!" she called. "Glad you could make it."

"I'm Tom." Tom shook her hand. "And this is my wife, Kim."

"Oh! I'm sorry. Just let me double-check my schedule so I know I don't have people waiting somewhere else." She practically dove into her bag and rummaged around, pushing aside old receipts and what looked like house photos. She pulled a smartphone out of her bag and clicked away at the keys. "Nope. It's you." She then pulled a sheet of paper out of her bag. "For this listing, right?" She looked at her notes.

Tom and Kim both nodded. "Yes, for now," said Tom. "We thought it would be a good place to start and we really like this house. I hope that's okay?"

"Of course. I understand love at first sight. I see it happen all the time. When you come upon the right house, you just know it. Let's have a look, shall we? Are these your boys? Lovely!"

Tommy Jr. and Ben ran over. "Is this the lady?" Tommy Jr. asked. "Will she give us the house? Tell her this is the one we want."

"Not yet, Tommy Jr.," Kim said. "We have to go inside and look around."

"Cool," Tommy Jr. said. "I'm gonna pick out my room." Ms. Davis had barely cracked open the door before the boys barreled past her and ran upstairs.

"It's all right," she said in reaction to Tom and Kim's mortified faces. "The house is empty. They can't break anything. Plus, this way we'll get to talk." She peered at the listing sheet.

"Well, this hasn't been on the market that long. And it's perfect for a family. Not many cul-de-sacs in this town, so it's always great when you can catch one right when it comes on. Would you like to have the swing set included?"

"Uh, we hadn't thought of it," Tom said, looking at Kim.

"Don't worry. That will come later. Let's have a look around. It's your basic Colonial. Hardwood floors. Open floor plan. You see how the kitchen flows nicely right into the family room."

It did. "We can all be in here and not be on top of each other," said Kim. "That would be great."

Ms. Davis continued, "Stainless steel appliances. Maple cabinets. Granite countertops. You like the fixtures and the backsplash?" She indicated the curved, pull-down nozzle in the kitchen sink and the blue and bronze mottled tiles framing the wall behind it. "Yes, it's very pretty," Tom murmured. He was trying to take it all in, but there seemed to be so much to look at. He noticed a set of sliding glass doors leading to a deck outside. Kim opened the doors of the cabinets, refrigerator, oven, and microwave. She slid a hand along the cool smooth granite as she moved about the kitchen. Tom was wondering whether their table would be too small for the room when he heard Ms. Davis raising her voice in the family room.

"And in here ..." she said. Tom and Kim looked at each other and scurried over to Ms. Davis. "We have a working fireplace. This home is heated with oil, so this is a nice feature to have to help lower your bills in the winter. Built-in window seat over there, and this room and the kitchen have been recently painted. It's a great space for family gatherings, don't you think?"

"Yes," Tom and Kim said in unison. They admired the high ceilings and the large windows looking out into the backyard. Ms. Davis kept talking, but Tom sidled out to check on the boys upstairs. He also just wanted to think, which he was finding really hard to do with Ms. Davis in the same room.

He found Tommy Jr. and Ben running down the hall.

"Look! We can go in a circle," Ben cried excitedly. We can go in this room and come out of that one. Tom followed them into a bedroom and through to a bathroom. It turned out the bathroom was shared with the bedroom next to it so it had a double set of doors. They emerged in the hall from the adjoining room.

"It looks like you've found your rooms, boys. How do you like them?"

"Can we have our own rooms, really?" Tommy Jr. asked.

"Yes. We can even paint them any color you like."

"I want mine purple," Ben shouted to Tom's chagrin.

"Come on, Ben, let's go through them again." Tommy Jr. pulled his little brother back to the rooms.

Tom found the master bedroom. It wasn't huge, but there was space for night tables next to the bed and chests of drawers, which they didn't have in their current bedroom. He opened a door and— what was this?—a walk-in closet. Kim might faint at the sight of it. He went over to one of the bedroom windows and leaned on the sill. He could hear the boys still chattering with excitement in the hall.

This really could be their home. But could they afford it? He and Kim had other dreams as well: family travel, college for the children, and maybe even a vacation house. And there were the dreams he had only partially shared with Kim because they were so big he was afraid they might scare her enough to discourage him. He wanted to start a business someday, maybe something he could build up enough to either sell for a big profit or pass on to their children if they wanted to run it. He also envisioned buying investment real estate so he and Kim would have a passive income in the years to come. They wouldn't have to work unless they wanted to. How great would that be? This was the future he wanted for himself and his family, and he wondered how many things they would have to give up or scale back to get into the house.

"I see you've discovered the master bedroom." Ms. Davis's voice cut right through Tom's thoughts. "You've probably noticed the double sinks in the bathroom, and the tile in the tub/shower combination. Walk-in closet, of course, and tray ceilings. The ceiling fan will be staying."

Kim nodded her approval at everything and she gave Tom a wide-eyed, happy look when she saw the closet. They viewed the remaining rooms, wrangling Tommy Jr. and Ben as they did so, and moved outside to walk around the entire yard.

"The boys can stay out here and enjoy the swing set," Ms. Davis suggested. "We'll be able to see them from the kitchen. Isn't that nice? Let's go back in and look at the offer."

Kim took Tom's hand and squeezed. The offer? They didn't think they'd have to deal with this so soon. Were they ready?

"So, what do you think of the house?" Ms. Davis asked as they gathered around the kitchen island. "It's obvious your little boys like it."

"Oh, yes, we love it," Tom began slowly. "We're just not sure how we'll proceed."

"Well, in this market you have to move quickly," Ms. Davis said. "This is a popular property. I have another family looking at it tomorrow and they could always put in an offer as well."

Tom could see Kim flinch and shift uncomfortably on her seat. He knew he had to take action. "Look, Ms. Davis, we really do like this house. What do we do?"

"This is your first house, isn't it? Don't worry. Look, we start by writing up an offer for the sellers. You'll be the first to have your foot in the door, so even if the people tomorrow make an offer, they'll have to beat yours." She began to pull some forms out of her bag and put pens in front of them. "Did you bring a checkbook?"

"Checkbook?" Now Tom was uneasy.

"Yes, for the deposit," Ms. Davis said airily. "You can make it out for $1,000. This is kind of like the down payment on your down payment. It shows the sellers that you're serious."

"But we don't even know yet if we can get a mortgage," Tom said, "or whom to go to for one."

"No problem." She handed Tom three business cards. "These are all mortgage originators. Call them and see what the current mortgage rates are. In the meantime, I'll put in your offer and see if the sellers accept it. Then we'll go from there."

Tom looked at Kim. She took his hand and nodded. Tom took out the checkbook. "Okay, let's do it."

Afterward, as they were driving home, Tom took Kim's hand again.

"I'll call the mortgage originators, but I'm not sure what to ask them. I guess she means that we should shop around for the lowest rate?"

"That is what it sounds like, but I'm not sure," Kim replied and sighed. "It will be all right. People have been buying houses since the beginning of civilization, haven't they?"

"Yes," Tom agreed. But he didn't tell her about the sinking feeling he had in the pit of his stomach. Maybe it was nothing.

When they pulled into the driveway of their apartment complex, they saw their neighbor John packing a set of golf clubs into the trunk of his car.

"Ah, back from the house hunt," he said. "How did it go?"

"We've put in an offer," Tom said, trying to sound confident and knowledgeable. "We'll see what happens."

"My, that was fast. You are really jumping into it," John said, a curious expression on his face.

"Well, we didn't want to lose the house," Tom said. "I guess we did move kind of quickly."

"Good luck," John said, getting into his car. "Let me know if you need anything. All right, Tom?"

"All right." Tom nodded, but with Ben tugging at his arm, he was obliged to keep going into the building. He watched as John's car rolled out of the parking lot.

"What does he do for a living?" Kim asked. "He doesn't seem to have nine to five hours."

"He must be retired, but it must be a nice retirement. He's always golfing and wearing nice clothes."

"Why is he living here?" Kim wondered. "He looks as if he could live anywhere. Why rent here?"

Tom heard her questions, but all he could think about was their offer on the house. This was supposed to be an exciting time, wasn't it? Why did he feel so lousy?

CHAPTER 3

What's Your Rate?

Tom sat at the kitchen counter with a brand new yellow legal pad and a pen. He placed the three business cards Ms. Davis had given him in a row next to the pad. He took a deep breath, picked up the phone, and dialed the number on the first card.

"Main Street Mortgage, can I help you?"

"Yes." Tom tried to sound confident. "I'm looking to apply for a mortgage and I'm calling to see what your rates are." He felt kind of silly asking the question. The truth was, he and Kim didn't really know what a good rate was. Why was he asking about rates when he had no point of reference to compare them?

"Just a moment, one of our loan officers will be with you shortly."

Tom listened to the elevator music as he doodled on the legal pad. After a minute or two he heard, "Mitchell Fusheade. Main Street Mortgage."

"Hi, I'm in the process of purchasing a home. I'm looking for a mortgage and I'd like to know what your rates are."

"Well, you're very smart to ask. Rates are in fact very good right now. Let's get your information." He proceeded to ask Tom for the price of the house, how much they planned to put down, and the amount of the mortgage he and Kim wanted. Tom thought that made sense. Mitchell Fusheade asked for their income amounts and how much credit card debt they had.

"Social Security number?" he asked.

"What?"

"I'll need your Social Security number, and your wife's."

Tom wasn't ready for this. "Look, I don't feel comfortable letting you pull my credit just yet. Quite frankly, I'm really trying to understand how this all works. Can you explain what your process is for helping people get a mortgage?"

"Sir, applying for a mortgage is a pretty straightforward business. The banks just want to know your debt-to-income ratio. If it's in line with their standards and if your credit is good, you should have no problem being approved."

"But I still have questions, like can I really afford the monthly payment, whatever it turns out to be, and accomplish my other goals for my family?"

"Well, sir, you know your finances better than anyone else. I can show you the figures, but you'll have to make the decision."

"Okay." Tom felt disheartened. How could he make the decision if he didn't know what to do with the information? "Look, I'll call you back. I have to think about this some more. Thanks." Actually, Tom wasn't sure if he wanted to call that guy back again. He seemed to be just a cheesy sales guy.

Tom hung up the phone and looked at the remaining two cards. If he called these guys, would he only get the same results? Maybe he was wasting his time. But then, he figured, Ms. Davis had given him three cards for a reason. Maybe it takes three to find the right one.

He called the number on the second card and heard a cheery voicemail greeting that directed him to leave a detailed message with his contact information. Something about the greeting made Tom feel more comfortable. He left a message explaining how they had submitted an offer and needed help so they could move forward. At first he worried that he was rambling, but figured the more information he gave the guy, the better prepared he'd be when he called Tom back. He was actually looking forward to talking with him, but unfortunately, he didn't call back.

On the third call, the loan officer answered the call himself. "This is Chip Becker. How can I help you?"

"Yes," Tom said, hesitating a moment. "I'm shopping for a mortgage. What are your rates?"

"Right now we have 30-year fixed rates at 5 percent and 7-year ARMs starting out in the 3 percent range, and if you pay points, you can get an even lower rate. Would you like to come in and talk about which mortgage might be right for you?"

"Uh, sure." Tom was uncertain what he would say in the meeting—he didn't even know what "points or ARMs" were, but he made an appointment for the following day.

He left for lunch early that afternoon and picked Kim up for their meeting with Chip Becker. They followed the driving directions Chip had provided and quickly found the building. Located on the main strip, it was an old farmhouse that had been converted into offices. Mr. Becker shared the facility with a chiropractor, a dentist, and a locksmith. A sign pointing to his upstairs office led Tom and Kim up a lopsided staircase carpeted in dingy gray. Tom had to duck to fit through the ancient doorframe. "This has to be a fire hazard," Tom mumbled.

"You found me. Good!" Mr. Becker greeted them very energetically. "Come in and sit down. Tell me about the house you're buying."

Tom and Kim smiled at each other. No one had asked them that yet. "It's great," Kim began. "It has a big yard and enough bedrooms for the kids ..."

Mr. Becker interrupted Kim. "Sounds awesome. How long do you plan to stay in it?"

"How long?" Tom scratched his head. "Well, I don't know. Maybe until the kids are grown. We don't plan on moving."

"Nobody plans on moving." Mr. Becker chuckled. "But it sounds as if you're going to stay in the house for at least five to seven years, right?"

"Uh, right," Tom replied.

"And you're probably wondering if you can afford the monthly payment, right?"

"Yes. How did you know?"

"Because that's what everyone worries about. People call and ask about rates, but what they really want to know is, 'How low can I make my monthly payment?' Here's an example. If you want a $300,000 mortgage, with a fixed rate of 5 percent on a 30-year mortgage, your monthly payment would be $1,610. But if you have an ARM, or an adjustable rate mortgage, at 4 percent, your monthly payment would be just $1,432. If you do interest only, the payment can be even lower. See how much of a difference that can be for your budget?"

"Wow, I do see," Tom said. Kim nodded.

"Now, you're probably planning to put down 20 percent, right?"

"No, we only have 10 percent to put down," Tom said. "Is that a problem?"

The loan officer frowned slightly but then smiled. "Oh, you will be subject to PMI ..."

"What's that?"

"Mortgage insurance. It's a small amount added to your monthly principal and interest payment. You keep paying it until you have 20 percent equity in the house."

A higher payment? Tom and Kim looked at each other. They didn't like the sound of that. "But how can we be sure it's affordable for us?" Tom asked. "We have a lot of plans, things we want to do. We don't want to put things off because we're held hostage by our mortgage payment each month."

"Don't worry about that. The bank won't let you take on more than you can handle. Let's crunch some numbers."

Just as he did with the first loan officer, Tom provided Mr. Becker with their income and debt figures and their other financial information.

"Yes, your debt-to-income ratio is fine."

Tom nodded. He still wasn't clear on what that ratio was supposed to be, but he figured he should be grateful that it was "fine" and acceptable to the banks. Just then his cell phone rang.

"Hello, it's Gwendolyn Davis with great news. The sellers like our offer on the home, but they will accept only if they get a pre-approval letter immediately."

"Really? Already? Uh, that's great."

"Did you call any of the loan officers I gave you?"

"We're in Mr. Becker's office right now."

"Wonderful! He's really good. Tell him you need a pre-approval letter and he'll take care of everything."

"Yeah, sure." But Tom wasn't sure he wanted this guy to take care of "everything."

He hung up the phone and told Kim and Mr. Becker the news. "Wow, okay," Kim said slowly.

"Well, now we really have to get moving." Mr. Becker began putting forms in from of them. "Did she say you need a pre-approval letter? I'll get to work on it immediately. We're on the clock now."

"What clock?" Tom asked.

"You only have a certain number of days after your offer has been accepted to secure a mortgage." Tom and Kim looked at each other and the knot of uneasiness began to form in Tom's stomach again. "What happens if we can't get a mortgage?"

"Well, usually if you can't follow through with the deal, you could lose your deposit."

"Lose our deposit!" It would be as if they had thrown $1,000 out of a window. Tom felt sick. Kim reached for his hand.

Mr. Becker said, "If it goes past the mortgage contingency date on the offer without securing a mortgage, you could lose your deposit. But don't worry. You're here and you have a head start on things. Let's get the pre-approval over to Gwendolyn."

He pushed two sets of papers toward Tom and Kim, and they began filling them out. Tom saw legal looking words fly past him, but he hardly knew what they meant. He decided to stick to what he knew and filled in the blanks on the pages as best he could. Kim did the same. By the time they left the office, their hands hurt from writing and their knees felt weak.

"Do you want to get something to eat?" Tom asked, looking at his watch. He had to get back to the office.

"After all that, it feels as if we can't afford lunch. Putting that 10 percent down will use up all of our savings, and Mr. Becker wants us to put 20 percent down. I wonder if there are any other programs where we can put less down?" Kim asked sadly. "Just drop me off at the apartment. I'm not hungry anyway."

"Come on, Kim, you have to eat for the baby's sake."

"I know. I'll get some crackers or something when I get home. I just can't eat anything right now."

An uncomfortable quiet filled the car on the drive home. Tom was thinking it must be good that this was all happening so quickly.

But he couldn't help feeling that it just seemed too fast and easy. When Tom pulled into the parking lot, Kim turned and kissed him. "I know it's going to be okay," she said. "We'll get through this together."

On the way back to the office, Tom stopped in their local coffeehouse to pick up a sandwich. As he waited for his order, he turned and saw his neighbor, John Randle, sitting at a table near the window. He was sipping a cup of coffee and reading the *Wall Street Journal*. When he looked up, he saw Tom and waved him over.

"Good to see you. Stopping in for a quick bite?"

"Yeah, I've got to get back to the office. Kim and I just got back from seeing someone about a mortgage."

"How did it go?"

"I think we got a good rate," Tom said, smiling weakly. He wasn't sure what that meant, but wasn't that what you were supposed to say? He could tell by the look on John's face, though, that he wasn't buying it.

"A good rate? Well, I guess that's part of the process."

Just then, Tom heard his order number called. "Gotta go. I'll talk to you later."

"Yes, see you later, Tom."

Tom turned away and then looked back quickly at John who seemed concerned. And Tom thought, just for a moment, that he'd seen John shaking his head.

Failure

A few days later a thick packet of papers arrived at the apartment via a delivery man. A note from Mr. Becker directed Tom to "discuss these with your wife and give me a call so we can plan your next step."

The long brown envelope had arrived much faster than Tom had expected. He took it over to the kitchen counter and pulled out the thick sheath of papers. On many of them were stickers with arrows and the words, "Sign here." Tom began to read, but what he saw just glancing over the numbers made his heart feel as if it wanted to stop. He saw a fast-approaching "commitment" date, a list of documentation he was required to procure and, most disturbing of all, a monthly payment that was much higher than what they had discussed with Mr. Becker, despite this being an ARM.

"What is it Tom? You look pale." Kim came in. She had just put the boys to bed.

"Here's the paperwork from Mr. Becker. You're not going to like it."

"What do you mean?" Kim came around the counter and began to look over the papers with Tom. Her eyes began to well up with tears. "But this is so much more than we talked about, isn't it? And what if the payment goes up after the rate adjusts? It's an ARM, right?"

"Yes," Tom said quietly.

"What are we going to do? We don't know what half of this stuff is about."

"I'll call him tomorrow."

"I don't understand. Is he trying to pull something on us?"

"I don't know, but I have to say, something about that guy bugged me."

"It did? Me too. Why didn't you say anything?"

"What was I supposed to say? We were sitting right there in front of him. Should I have said, 'I'm sorry. You seem like a jerk. We're getting out of here.'"

"Well, yeah. This is our family we're talking about, and our savings, and our future."

"You think I don't know that? You think I enjoy feeling like a total idiot in this whole thing with so much at stake?"

"I just thought …"

"Thought what?" Tom tried to keep his voice level. He didn't want to wake the children, but he couldn't help the tension gripping his throat.

"You said you were going to figure this out. I can't do it. I've got enough on my plate with the boys and the new baby."

"Are you saying this is my fault?"

"I'm saying we need to figure this out. We could probably make this payment if you asked for a raise at work."

"Yeah, and we could definitely make it if you went back to work, at least part-time."

"What about day care? Do you have any idea how much that costs? And if the children are in day care, how do we know our family values will be instilled in them? Someone else will be raising our kids."

The look on Kim's face made Tom desperately want to take back his words. If Kim went back to work, they would be turning away from everything they wanted for their family, even before they ever thought of buying a home. Both Tom and Kim had been raised in families with parents who worked long hours and family lives that only really existed when they were on vacation. They had promised each other that their family would be different, that their kids would always have one parent at home for as long as they needed. Now Tom felt that he was going back on that promise. Kim began to cry.

"I'm sorry," he said, pulling her into his arms. "I'm really sorry. Look we're both dog-tired. Let's just go to bed. I'll call this guy in the morning."

But as he lay in bed that night, Tom couldn't sleep. He and Kim had never argued like that before. He couldn't believe how quickly things had changed. Just a few days ago he felt on top of the world. Now he felt so low he might as well be homeless. Kim was counting on him to take the lead on this. It was time for him to step up to the plate.

When he called Mr. Becker the next day, Tom was determined to get some clear answers.

"Don't worry," Mr. Becker said too heartily. "We'll take care of everything. We are the loan closing experts."

"Don't worry?" Tom thought. "Why do I worry more when he says that?"

Mr. Becker went on. "That's just the potential monthly payment, and it's based on the rate that was available the day these papers were drawn up. Mortgage rates change daily and you haven't locked yours in yet."

"We have to lock in a rate? But you didn't tell us that before."

"Well, you can't really lock in a rate until we put the paperwork through."

"I'm also wondering …" Tom hesitated, "is an adjustable rate mortgage really right for us?"

"Well, the payment is lower, and you told me that's what you wanted, but we can always do a fixed rate. Is that what you want?

Now Tom was bewildered. How was he supposed to know what they needed? And Mr. Becker wasn't helping. Then he thought of something. "Wait a minute, you need more paperwork from us?"

"Yes, we'll need your tax forms, bank statements, all the documents that confirm what you put in the application. Didn't you see the list I sent?"

"In that huge package? There must have been seventy pages." Tom felt as if something was wringing his stomach.

"Look, I'm just trying to make this happen for you as quickly as possible. I thought you really wanted this house?"

"I did. We do. But we also wanted to talk to you about the other things we want to do like making sure we have enough left over to get a second home someday if we want one, saving for our retirement, and sending the kids to college. I guess I want to look at the big picture. We would also like to purchase some investment property and potentially build a real estate portfolio someday. How will buying this house impact all of that?"

Tom heard Mr. Becker clear his throat on the other end of the line. "That's not really my job."

"It's not?"

"No. My job is to get you into a mortgage."

Tom froze. He could feel the picture of his kids playing in the yard of the house slipping away, but he couldn't keep going on with this process, not like this. They could stand to lose even more. "I'm sorry," he said slowly. "This is my fault. Kim and I need a little time to think and discuss this. Thanks for all your help." Tom hung up the phone.

He drove home that evening in a daze. A thousand-dollar deposit was gone, just like that. Tom felt stupid and ashamed. He hardly knew how he would face Kim and drove an extra long route home so he could put it off as long as possible.

When he walked through the door, Kim could tell something was wrong. She smiled and kept their conversation on the boys and their school activities. As they looked at each other, they both knew that what they had to talk about would have to wait until the boys were in bed. In fact, Kim and Tom waited until they themselves were in bed before Tom gave her all the details.

Kim listened, stared at the ceiling, and nodded. "We can't go through with this," she said quietly.

"That's what I was thinking too."

"But what about our deposit?"

"I think we're going to lose it. We just have to accept that. I don't know. I guess it's a learning experience."

"An expensive one."

"Yes."

Kim turned over and said nothing more. In a few minutes she was asleep. Tom, however, stayed up and replayed the scenes of the past few days over and over again in his head. He wondered what he could have done differently.

CHAPTER 5

Tom's Nightmare

The alarm had gone off much too soon. Then Tom remembered. He had the breakfast shift this morning at the restaurant—4 a.m. to 9 a.m. He had begged the manager for the extra hours and crafted a careful excuse so he could be a little late to his day job.

He reached out for Kim, but she wasn't there. She must have spent another night on the floor in the kids' room. She didn't like it when he woke up so early. As a matter of fact, she didn't like a lot of the things he did lately. It seemed as if everything they said turned into a fight. And they always fought over the same thing: money.

Tom went into the bathroom, shaved, and brushed his teeth. Then he pulled on his clothes, grabbed his bag, and walked out. He carefully turned the doorknob of the other bedroom. Kim lay on a pile of sofa cushions in the space between the baby's bed and the wall. Everyone was still sleeping peacefully. But Tom could hear Tommy Jr.'s voice cutting through his mind.

"Why can't we go to Disney World like all the other kids? Everyone is going away for vacation. Why can't we? We never get to do anything."

"I told you, when you can pay for it, we can go."

"Why do I have to pay for it? I'm not a grown up!"

"Yeah, but you're the one who wants to go."

"That's not fair!"

Then Ben piped in, "I hate you. You're not nice."

"You don't play with us anymore. It's like you don't live here anymore."

Tom sighed and closed the door quietly. They would have to be up in a few hours. He was sad, but he couldn't blame them. It seemed all any of them did was work. He worked long hours. The kids did their work at school and came home. He and Kim couldn't afford to put them in activities.

At least they were going away soon. He started the car. They would go to Kim's sister's house for the break. In fact, that was what they always did—go to someone else's house. Of course, they had no room for family stuff in the apartment.

When he got to work, Tom sat in the car for a full five minutes. He went through this every time. He always went through this period of disbelief—disbelief that he was about to walk into a McDonald's, not to order a hamburger and fries, but to work.

Disheartened, Tom bowed his head and took a deep breath. As he looked up, in a split second of recognition he thought he saw his father's tired eyes looking back at him in the rearview mirror.

Suddenly the scene changed, and Tom saw Kim sitting in an office listening to a man behind a desk.

"And he had no life insurance? None at all?"

"No," Kim said. Her eyes were red and she seemed older by several years.

"Your husband left behind substantial debts. I'm sorry to say you might have to sell your home to pay them off."

"But we don't own a home."

The man shook his head. "Then we'll have to figure out something else. You'll have to declare bankruptcy, most likely, and get a job to keep your household going. Have you considered what you will do?"

Kim cried openly now. "I have no idea. I can't even think straight right now. I can't believe Tom is gone. He said he had a headache, just a headache. And then that morning I couldn't wake him up. What are we going to do? What are we going to do? How will I take care of the kids?"

"Oh my God! Kim!" Tom wanted desperately to reach out to her. "Kim, I'm sorry. I'm sorry I did this to us. I'm sorry."

Tom woke up in a cold sweat, his fingers clutching the blankets around him. He turned quickly to see if he had woken Kim, but she was still asleep beside him. He ran his hands through his hair. I can't let that happen, Tom thought. "I can't let that happen to my family."

John and the Core 7
A Point in the Right Direction

The next morning, Tom was pretty much useless at work and he knew it. He had a hard time focusing, but at the same time he knew he had to make the call that would confirm his failure. He would tell Ms. Gwendolyn Davis that he and Kim had to pull out of the deal. He was pretty sure he would have to forfeit their $1,000 deposit.

What he didn't expect was Gwendolyn Davis's behavior.

"What do you mean you need to think more about the process? You seemed pretty certain when we saw the house."

"I know, but we're new to this. We told you that. It would help to have more guidance about the financial part."

"Guidance from who? Me? I gave you people to go to for a mortgage and Mr. Becker got you that pre-approval letter pretty quick, didn't he?"

"I know, but that's all you did. You just gave us three cards without any discussion of what we had to look for."

"Look, I'm obligated to give out three cards, all right? Otherwise I have too much liability."

Tom wasn't finding the conversation helpful. "I'm sorry, Ms. Davis. What about our deposit?"

"I'll look into it, but don't expect the sellers to be forgiving. You wasted their time too, and they deserve to keep the deposit if you ask me." She hung up the phone.

At lunchtime, Tom found himself hungry and just a bit angry. "I'll go out to eat," Tom thought. "I need to get out of here and think."

He went back to the same café he had visited after meeting with Mr. Becker that first time. And just as he had before, he saw his neighbor, John Randle, sitting by himself near the window enjoying a cup of coffee.

"Can I join you?" Tom asked, his sandwich and coffee in hand.

"Please do. It's good to see you, Tom." John pulled out a chair and smiled, but then he frowned slightly. "Forgive me for saying so, my friend, but you don't look so good."

"Didn't get much sleep last night," Tom confessed. "Things aren't going well with buying the house. I just pulled out of the deal."

John nodded with a look of concern. "Did you put a deposit down?"

"Yes. We're probably going to lose it too." Tom sighed and leaned back in his chair. "I'm at my wit's end, John. I just don't know enough about the process and I don't know whom to trust or what to do."

"I see."

"You are a renter, John. Tell me, if you were to decide to buy a home, who would you go to for advice?"

"That's not true, Tom. I actually own the building we live in and several others. I moved into my place a few years ago to be closer to my grandchildren after my wife passed away."

Tom nearly spit out his coffee. "Oh my God, so you are my landlord? I thought it was Chris. That's who I send my rent to."

"He's my son. He manages all of my properties. I spend my time managing a charity I started after my wife's passing. I was fortunate to have the finances and a plan, which allowed me to grieve for her properly without having to worry about money. But after a while, I knew I needed a reason to get up in the morning. That's why I started a charity in her name."

"Oh, I didn't know." Tom felt stupid, and now John probably thought he was stupid as well. Still, he had to ask, "Well, maybe, do you think, maybe you could help me?"

John took a long sip from his coffee and looked at Tom closely. "I'm not one to give advice lightly, Tom, especially in matters like this, which I take very seriously. I'd be happy to help, but you have to promise me that you will listen carefully and follow through with everything I tell you. Do we have a deal?"

Tom was starting to feel hopeful. "Yes. I promise, I will."

"First, let me ask you some questions. Was this house just about finding a bigger place to live?"

"No. It's funny. That's how my thinking started, but when I really started to see my family in the house, I could see it meant something more. I felt we were going to build something—a different way of life, I guess. And the house itself would be kind of like a foundation for building our financial future."

"Good. You're a smart man, Tom. You might not feel great about yourself right now, but after you see the big picture, you will feel better. I am sure of it. I figured you were someone who could see the big picture."

Tom smiled with relief at the compliment but then blanched when he heard John's next question.

"Let me ask you, Tom. Wouldn't you agree that this is probably the largest single investment that you and Kim have ever made?

"Well, yes, absolutely."

"Well, I can also tell you that buying your first home is going to trigger many other financial responsibilities in your life. Would you agree with that?"

"Yes."

"Don't you think it should take longer than a few days to build the future?"

"Well, yes."

"It felt kind of fast, didn't it, the way all this house stuff was moving along?"

"Yes, it did. The whole process we just went through was kind of fast and confusing, like a ride on a roller coaster."

"That's okay, it's understandable to be uneasy with your first big purchase. Who was advising you? Who was standing up for you and keeping your vision of the future in mind? I guess I'm asking, who was on your team?"

"No one," Tom replied. "It seemed everyone involved represented their own or someone else's interests. They barely asked about ours."

"That was the big missing piece, Tom. You had no one representing you. Now you have finally asked me for help and I will point you in the right direction."

Tom sat up straight. "Yes, absolutely!"

"Look, Tom, what I'm about to share with you is not the easiest advice to follow. I follow it today and I can guarantee you that if you stick with it, you will be able to build that future you want. Here's the thing: in order to create a sound financial future for your family, you'll need to have a team full of people who are all focused on your vision and your long-term financial health. And I want to stress 'long-term' because short-term strategies rarely work. People drastically overestimate what they can do in a year, but drastically underestimate what they can do in a decade or two. You need a team of at least seven advisors who can help you examine every aspect of your financial life."

"Seven?" Tom marveled at the number. "Is it really necessary to have seven people all working for me?"

"Yes, it is," John assured him. "These are the most important advisors you'll ever have. Some will play a larger role than others in the purchase of your first home, and others will have a more active role in other major financial decisions in your life. But it is important to get your team in place as soon as possible. Why not do it right now, to help with what is probably your first major financial decision?"

"That makes sense," Tom said, "but it seems a lot of people are involved. Is seven too many? My dad always said that too many cooks spoil the soup."

John nodded. "I understand your thinking, but this group has a system that they use with every client they work with, that incorporates the seven professionals in a turnkey fashion. Besides a realtor and a mortgage originator, you'll also be working with a real estate attorney, a financial advisor, a home owner's insurance agent, an estate planning attorney and an accountant."

Tom carefully wrote down each team member and looked at the list. "Aren't some of these redundant? Surely the accountant can serve as my financial advisor as well?"

"In order for your people to do their jobs well, you'll have to let each member of the team focus on what they do best," said John. "For instance, if you had a heart condition, you would not go to a general practitioner. You would see a cardiologist. Of course, this is not life or death in the same way, but I think your financial help is almost as important as your health. You'll learn more about what the team members do as you speak with each one."

The length of the list still made Tom feel overwhelmed. Looking for the mortgage guy had been bad enough. Now he had to go through all that times seven? "Okay, but how will I find all these people?" he asked John.

"You will work with the same team I use. I've worked with most of them for years."

Tom breathed a huge sigh of relief. He trusted John and he knew any name he shared with him had to be good.

"We'll start with the realtor. I want to be sure that you two make contact as soon as possible." John pulled out his smartphone and asked Tom for his e-mail address. Then he tapped out an e-mail that read:

Chuck meet Tom, Tom meet Chuck. Tom and his wife are looking to buy their first home, and I told him he would receive great benefit from working with you, so I wanted to put you two together. I told Tom that you are the best, and it would be a ton of value to him to go through your buyer meeting at your office. I put you both on this e-mail so you two can connect.

"Okay," John said when he had finished. "That should get you started."

Tom was beginning to feel excited. "What about the others?"

"Chuck will get you started."

"He will? He knows them all?"

"Yes. Remember, my advisors are a true team. They all know each other and they all know my goals. That way, they can work together to help me accomplish them. They will do the same for you."

Tom was impressed—and hungry. He felt so much better that he was suddenly ravenous. He bit into his sandwich.

"But Tom," John took another sip of his coffee, "you're going to have to be really committed to your goals. Some of the work you'll have to do to get there won't be easy. These people can help you, but only you can take the lead in your own life."

"All right. I know I can do that. I have to—my family needs me to."

"Yes, that's true."

"John?" Tom put his sandwich down and reached across the table to shake John's hand. "Thank you. Really, thank you so much."

"You're welcome, Tom. I know where you're coming from. I've been there, too. I'm happy to use my experiences to help you move on."

Tom nodded gratefully. "By the way, what is the charity you started? The one in your wife's name?"

"It's a foundation for cancer research. My wife died of cancer, and I was devastated. The charity has really given me purpose to carry on her memory. We started the foundation five years ago, and we've been able to fund grants to research facilities all over the world. It's really given me a purpose. I'm glad you asked."

As he drove back to the office, Tom was grateful for how much better he felt. He couldn't wait to call Kim and tell her about his talk with John. He also couldn't help thinking that some small prayer inside him had been answered. And he was truly grateful for that as well.

Review

CHAPTER 6

Referral is given to Realtor. The best introductions are made via email with both the Realtor and client copied.

CHAPTER 7

The Real Estate Agent

By the time Tom got back to his office, he discovered he already had an e-mail from the realtor John had contacted in the coffee shop. The return e-mail read:

John, thank you so much for connecting me with Tom. As always, I appreciate your excellent referrals. Tom, what would be good number for me to call to reach you? Looking forward to speaking with you, and hearing how I can be of help.

Thx-Chuck Stone

"Wow, that was fast," Tom thought as he responded to Chuck's e-mail. But somehow he didn't mind speed this time. He really wanted to get good advice as soon as possible. When Chuck called that afternoon, he seemed warm and engaging.

"Let's set a time to talk about your search and the process," Chuck said. "When is a good time for you to come to my office?"

Tom pulled out his calendar and set a date. He was glad, but he was also cautiously reserved. He didn't want to set his hopes too high. He wanted good things to happen in this meeting with Chuck, John's realtor. But since he didn't know what a good relationship with a realtor looked like, he didn't know what to expect. All he could do was hold hands with Kim and dive into this new pool.

When they walked into the office building for their appointment, Tom could tell this would be a different experience. The reception area was bright and clean and the people coming in and out were well-dressed and professional. A young woman in a pink blouse and brown skirt greeted them warmly.

"Good morning. You must be Tom and Kim. You're here to see Chuck?"

"Yes, good morning." Tom and Kim shook hands with the woman.

"I'm Kaitlin. Let me show you into the conference room. Chuck will be with you shortly."

The room contained a long mahogany table surrounded by cushy, cloth-covered chairs with wheels. Tom leaned back in his seat and caught a whiff of fresh-brewed coffee. Before he could ask for a cup, Kaitlin offered them some.

"Would you like some coffee? How do you take it?"

She returned with the cups and Tom and Kim sipped at the steaming drinks and smiled at each other. "This already feels a whole lot better, doesn't it?" Kim said.

"One hundred times better."

They had taken just a few sips when Chuck came in, dressed in a crisp white shirt with a blue and purple striped tie. He carried a tablet computer that he placed on the table before offering his hand to Tom and Kim. "Good morning, Tom. Good morning, Kim. It's great to meet you."

Tom was thinking he already liked Chuck's warm, open demeanor as they all sat down. "You've met Kaitlin. I also have several other members on my team such as Gale, my transaction coordinator, whom you will meet once we have a property under agreement. I just want you to know that every single person in this office is here to serve you."

Tom and Kim looked at each other and smiled. "That sounds good to us," Tom said.

"My team and I really want to understand your needs and be a resource for you, your family members, and your friends."

Tom and Kim nodded as Chuck went on.

"First, I would like to explain to you how I work and what makes me different. Most realtors spend the majority of their time and resources prospecting for new business. They do things such as cold calling, door knocking, advertising, and direct mail. I don't do any of that. I work 100 percent by referral and devote myself to serving the needs of my clients before, during, and after each transaction."

"After the transaction?" Tom asked.

"Yes. I can help you evaluate the benefit or value of home improvements to make sure they make sense. All I ask is that while I'm working for you, you refer me to people of comparable quality to yourself, who are looking for the type of service I provide, and who would appreciate the same level of attention. You see, as long as you and my other clients keep referring, I don't have to prospect for new business like everyone else, and I can pour my time and energy into serving you. That means it does not make a difference to me if you buy in two months or in two years. I just want to make sure I do a good job for you. Does that make sense?"

"Yes." Tom nodded. He really liked what Chuck said because it meant he had a stake in his and Kim's well-being. It added to Chuck's trust factor.

"So let me start by asking you a question. If I could wave a magic wand and have everything work out perfectly for you, what does that look like?"

"We've been thinking about that." Tom looked at Kim. "You see, we're going to have our third child soon."

"Congratulations!"

"Thanks. Well, we want to have a good home life for our kids."

"Good home life." Chuck nodded. "What does that look like? Be as specific as you can."

"It means I can be at home with the children and not have to work," Kim said. "Tom and I both grew up with working parents and we just want our children to have the experience of more time with us."

"Yes, and where we live now, we barely have enough room to think straight," Tom added. "We want to live in a place where we can spread out a little and be more relaxed. The boys are really on top of each other in their room."

"How old are your sons?"

"Six and four years old," Kim replied.

"So you will need a yard, right?" Tom and Kim nodded. "Good to know," Chuck said, typing a note into his computer. "We can figure out how many years until you need to worry about being in good schools. Okay, what else?"

"Well, we know a house is a big investment," said Tom, "But we'd like to be able to do other things with our money too. We want to travel with our kids and be able to save money for their college. We don't want our house payment to overwhelm us so much that we can't build a real estate portfolio."

"Yes, and maybe get a second home," said Kim.

Before they knew it, they had poured everything out to Chuck. They told him all of their hopes and dreams. They talked about where they wanted to live and how Kim might go back to school someday and get a graduate degree and how Tom might want to start a business because he wanted to leave something for the kids. The funny thing was, Tom now felt he could see it all happening and he was feeling warm and happy. He could see it in Kim's face too because she was glowing with pride as she talked about the boys. Then he wondered if they were getting carried away.

"Um, I'm sorry Chuck, but how will this help us right now? Are we still going to look at some houses?"

"Has that been your experience with the other agents you worked with? They just wanted to show you houses?"

"Well, we only looked at one house with one agent," Tom said sheepishly. "And, as I told you over the phone, we'll probably lose our deposit there. That's why we wanted to start over with you. We don't want to overspend because there are so many other things we want to do."

"Did you tell that to the other people?"

"Yes, but it seemed they were not listening. We didn't know if we could afford what we were buying, and no one seemed to be able to help us with that. It was as if they only cared about earning their commission."

Chuck said, "That's because that agent worked for the seller. I work for you. I told John I would take good care of you, so we are going to start at the very beginning and I am going to explain to you how this process actually works. I will be with you every step of the way."

"We really liked that house," said Kim sadly. "And now we're going to lose the house and our money. Tom and I feel terrible."

"I understand," Chuck said. "The whole experience sounds very disappointing. But let me assure you that there are plenty of houses out there. In fact, we have a saying in the real estate world, 'The right property comes around about once a week.' That's just how it works out. But it will never be the right house unless it fits in with the rest of your life goals."

Tom reached for Kim's hand and squeezed it. He could tell that Chuck was listening to what they were saying.

"So let me reiterate," Chuck went on, "You're looking for an affordable home in a nice neighborhood, with good schools, where you'll be able to raise your family and create memories while not being overburdened by the mortgage payment. And you would like to eventually buy some investment property, and possibly a second home. Is that right?"

Tom and Kim nodded eagerly. "Yes, that's exactly right," Tom replied. Chuck said, "We won't lose sight of your investment property goal. In fact, I'll create an *investment property spreadsheet** for us to use after we're done with this purchase. It will help us figure out an investment property strategy, factoring in rates of return, depreciation, and how it will all fit in with your overall investment plan. But for right now, the first thing I would like to do, is have you meet my lender."

"Lender?" Tom asked. "But we haven't found a house yet. Are we going to look at some houses?"

"I'm sorry, Tom," Chuck said. "Let me take a step back here. We want to make sure you get pre-approved before we start looking at homes. I want to make sure that you have no stress, and that you know exactly what you can afford, so you can concentrate and relax. We want to know that you are looking at the right property. That's one of your questions that went unanswered before, right?"

"Yes." Tom nodded vigorously.

"My lender will help you with that. His name is Marc and he is a mortgage planner. He will help you incorporate the mortgage you select into your overall financial strategy, which includes your

---

*   For investment property spreadsheet go to *www.whats-your-rate.com*

long- and short-term financial and investment goals as well as your payment, equity, and cash flow objectives."

"But the guy we worked with before said that wasn't his job," said Tom, not hiding the surprise in his voice. "And honestly, I didn't think to ask him until it was too late. I thought I was just supposed to ask about the rates he offered."

Chuck smiled understandingly. "Yes, that's how most clients start out. Rates are important, but what's more important is making the right financial decisions and structuring the mortgage properly. Rates change every day, like a stock, based on the secondary market. Mortgage-backed securities are contained in the secondary bond market. These bonds travel in ranges and can change multiple times per day based on economic activity. Marc will explain this in more detail, which is why I always have my clients speak with him a few days before they even consider making an offer. I always make sure I give him enough time to do his research to find the right loan, make sure my clients qualify, and understand the process. This is so he can issue a 'real' pre-approval.

"A pre-approval makes an offer much stronger, and all of the good real estate agents that are selling homes know this. There are many times that an offer with a pre-approval will be accepted over a higher priced bid with only a pre-qualification."

Tom was shocked but pleased. "This is a very different experience," he thought. "I already feel that we're getting some great guidance."

"After we have an accepted offer," Chuck said. "I would like to introduce you to my attorney."

"A real estate attorney, right?" Tom asked. "Another one of the team of advisors?"

"I see John filled you in really well. Yes, he's another key member of the team. He is very professional and, together with Marc's mortgage team, will watch your very important contingency dates." Chuck pulled out a chart showing the *process and timelines.**

"Our job is to keep you safe. The most important contingency date is your mortgage commitment. The mortgage commitment is the date when we need to know that your financing is approved. We need a clean commitment from the lender, and the attorney and I want to review it at least one day in advance because it may be subject to conditions."

"Oh, yes, we already know about that one," Tom said. "That's the date when I can lose my deposit, right? I think we've already been there."

"Yes," said Chuck. "If you pass this date and are unable to obtain the mortgage, you can lose the 5 to 10 percent that is typically required as a deposit when you sign the purchase and sale. A seller usually wants $1,000 with the offer, and the full balance of 5 percent at purchase and sale. It sounds as if you started down that road. I will have my attorney look into that for you. The great thing about having an attorney is that he is representing you and will help manage the process. You and your family will be very well protected."

Now Tom was really beginning to understand. This was what John meant about having people on his side looking out for his interests. He felt Kim squeeze his hand and when he turned to her, he could see a tear welling up in her left eye. She felt the same way. She was imagining her kids playing in the yard of their new home. They just knew something good had to come of all this with so many great people helping them.

---

* For a copy of the process and timelines go to *www.whats-your-rate.com*

As if he could hear their thoughts, Chuck went on to explain, "This is why I like all of my clients to use my team. It's the best way to manage the whole process. If anything unexpected pops up, I know that these people will do whatever they possibly can to make things right. Also, I can always get up-to-date information, reach them during off hours, and most importantly, know that I am dealing with the truth during the transaction. The only unsolvable problems I've had during transactions are when my clients do not use my team."

"But the other realtor we worked with just gave us three cards and said we had to shop around. She said she would get a lot of flak for just recommending one person," Tom said.

Chuck shook his head. "I don't agree with handing out three cards because it's too confusing for clients. They hesitate and don't know how to move forward. As a buyer's agent, I have only your interests at heart. I have never been able to find a law against recommending one person. I would never steer a client to anyone without reason, but I don't want to encourage shopping either. A good lender should always be competitive."

Chuck turned to his computer and began typing. "I am going to e-mail my lender right now to make the introduction," he said as he worked. "I want you to be fully pre-approved as soon as possible, before we begin to look at properties."

"Pre-approvals are usually fast anyway, aren't they?" Tom asked.

"They can be," Chuck said, still typing. "But I want to make sure we get a "real" pre-approval before we even consider making an offer. Let's be certain that we are going to get approved for the loan, and that you are 100 percent comfortable with the purchase of your future home."

Chuck then handed Tom and Kim a portfolio folder that had Chuck's company logo on the front. "I want you to be prepared.

Here is my *homebuyer packet** that outlines the whole process. It gives you a rough estimate of closing costs, a copy of all the other forms so you will not be surprised when the time comes, and a check-list to give you an idea of some of the documents that the lender may need: your tax returns, your W-2s, all of your statements for all of your asset accounts, things like that. You'll want to get all this paperwork together as quickly as possible, but make sure to be thorough. I'd rather see you take more time to gather everything upfront."

Tom and Kim stared at the folder as though Chuck had handed them a golden ticket. Tom was impressed with Chuck's preparation and how he so obviously wanted them to be prepared as well. That Becker guy, and Gwendolyn Davis, Tom could see now, had just wanted to push them into buying that property right away. Looking for a house this time was going to be very different—maybe even fun—if he and Kim knew so much up front. He couldn't wait to get home and go through the folder with her.

Chuck continued typing. "I'm sending an e-mail introducing my lender now so you'll be able to connect. His name is Marc Malone from the Malone Group." The e-mail read:

> *As I mentioned today, Marc Malone from the Malone group is the lender we use. He is a mortgage planner and will focus on the best structure for your loan, also factoring the mortgage into your overall financial plan. Bill from his office will reach out to you. They ask for all of your financial documents up front so they can get a complete picture and not miss any important information.*
>
> *Thx-Chuck*

As if he had read Tom's mind again, Chuck said, "Now let's set a time to look at some properties. I'm also going to set you up on

---

* For a copy of the homebuyer packet go to *www.whats-your-rate.com*

my property finder. As soon as I get the pre-approval amount from Marc, we can get an idea of properties that you may be interested in. I'll forward them on to you as they come in and you can let me know which ones you want to see when we go out. Just take your time and enjoy. We won't really be focused on a purchase the first time we go out. I just want you to get a sense for price and space.

"This is a process of elimination, not selection. Every time you see a property you don't like, it will help us know when we find the right one. We really want to narrow down exactly what you are looking for. I don't want you writing an offer on any property until we have a good sense of the market. When you look at properties online, I want you to grade them A, B, C, or D. We are going to see the As, Bs, and Cs. I also want to give my lender enough time so we can have the firmest pre-approval possible."

Now Tom and Kim were really excited. As they left Chuck's office, they wanted to make sure he knew how much they were looking forward to working with him.

"I can't thank you enough," Tom said, shaking Chuck's hand.

"Well, we haven't done anything yet." Chuck laughed warmly.

"No, you've really done a lot already. Kim and I feel so much better about this. That's worth so much to us."

Back at the apartment building, Tom and Kim bypassed their own door and went straight to John's apartment and rang the doorbell.

John opened the door. "Well, what a nice surprise. And what big smiles. I see you've met Chuck."

"Yes," said Kim. "We just wanted to thank you. The process is already so different. We're so excited about it."

"I see what you mean now about the importance of working with people who care about our goals," Tom said. "Thank you."

"You can thank me later." John smiled. "There's still a long way to go. But you can always come back and ask me questions if you need me."

"What a nice man," Kim said as Tom turned the key in their door.

"Yes," Tom agreed. "He feels kind of like a mentor."

Kim laughed. "I was actually going to say a guardian angel."

Tom smiled, but before he could respond he heard the babysitter call out, "Tommy Jr., Ben! Mommy and Daddy are home," and he lost his train of thought as the boys came tumbling out of their room.

Review

CHAPTER 6

Referral is given to Realtor. The best introductions are made via email with both the Realtor and client copied.

CHAPTER 7

Realtor makes appointment at the office.

Buyer meeting at the Realtor's office.

Realtor refers the Mortgage Originator.

CHAPTER 8

The Home Search Begins
Getting Ahead of the House

The next day Tom opened his e-mail to find a communication from Marc's production manager, Bill Pappas. Tom noticed the e-mail was in reply to Chuck's e-mail introducing Marc and the members of his team. "Wow," he thought, "They really do want to keep everyone in the loop."

The e-mail read:

Dear Tom and Kim,

My name is Bill. I'm a member of Marc's team. On behalf of Marc and all of us on his team, thank you for the opportunity to assist you.

Chuck asked that I touch base to schedule a time for you and Marc to discuss your mortgage financing options. I also tried reaching you at the number Chuck provided, but got your voicemail. I left a message.

Marc conducts mortgage-planning sessions Monday–Friday from one to six. Please let me know what day and time works best for you, and I'll set that aside in his schedule.

I've taken the liberty of attaching the Pre-consultation Worksheets.* They consist of the application, mortgage-planning analysis, and a document checklist along with your permission to run your credit. We ask all of our clients to complete the application and questionnaire prior to speaking with Marc.

Please e-mail or fax me the completed forms in addition to the following items from the list:

- W-2s for the last two years
- If you are self-employed, receive commission income, are employed by relatives, or receive rental income, please send all pages of signed 1040s for the last two years
- Bank/asset statements (all pages, even blank) for the last two months
- Pay stubs for the last two pay periods

We realize providing this documentation up-front may be tedious, but it's the only way Marc can ensure he doesn't miss an important piece of information and is able to issue your pre-approval letter with little or no conditions.

Please feel free to e-mail or call me if you have any questions.

Best regards,

Bill

PS: I've also attached a document entitled "Do's and Don'ts When Applying for a Mortgage" for your review. It has some very useful suggestions of what you should and should not do at this stage in the mortgage process.

Tom was impressed by Bill's e-mail, but despite Chuck's warning, he was a little concerned about all of the documentation he was asked

---

* For a copy of the Pre-consultation Worksheets go to *www.whats-your-rate.com*

to provide. He decided that because Bill had told him to feel free to call him, he would do just that.

After introductions, the first thing that Bill did was to congratulate Tom on his decision to work with Chuck. "We've been working with Chuck for several years and he does an amazing job for all of his clients. You are in very good hands, Tom. Now, were you able to open all the documents I e-mailed you?"

"Yes I was. Thank you for that."

"Not a problem. Did you have any questions about them? I know it can be a bit daunting providing all of the information we ask for up-front, but let me assure you it's more about us than it is about you. Marc wants to be able to research your options beforehand and make certain he advises you to the best of his ability. The last thing he wants to do is overpromise then underdeliver. Having all your documentation up-front prevents that from happening."

Tom remembered that was what Chuck had said. If this were coming from anyone else, he probably would have written it off as sounding canned. But Bill's professional manner confirmed for Tom that the team members knew what they were doing. It also showed that they had collaborated, and were very familiar with each other's process.

Bill continued, "Marc takes a different approach from most lenders. He wants to make sure the loan you select is integrated into your long- and short-term financial and investment goals as well as your payment, equity, and cash-flow objectives."

After hearing this, Tom decided he felt much better about providing the documents.

"I'd like to schedule a time for you to discuss your options with Marc," Bill said. "Do you have a particular date and time that works best for you, Tom? I can set that aside in Marc's schedule for you."

After scheduling the meeting, Bill said, "You're all set, Tom. Just be sure to e-mail or fax the documents to me prior to your meeting with Marc."

Tom hesitated. He was sure Mr. Becker had already pulled a report for him before. He had heard that multiple checks on his file could hurt his credit score. He felt himself starting to worry when he stopped himself. "Wait a minute," he thought. "This is what my team is for. I'll just ask."

"The other guy we used before already pulled my credit recently. Will it hurt my credit score for you to do it again, so soon?"

"Good question, Tom. No, it won't. There is something called the 'shotgun' effect in credit scoring that allows for multiple credit checks for a permissible purpose—in this case mortgages—over a short period of time with the resulting inquiries affecting your credit score as if it were pulled only once."

"Oh, I didn't know that." Tom felt better again. He thought it was funny how asking the right question could help so much.

Tom was surprised by the attention to detail. The other lenders hadn't asked for documentation up-front. They just started talking about the loan right then and there. But when he thought about this, Tom realized that by filling out the application, completing the questionnaire, providing all of the documentation, and allowing Marc to research his options, he would understand what was important to him and Kim. Mr. Becker certainly hadn't. Then he remembered what John had said about going through the work and listening carefully to his team. This is what he meant. So Tom had to get everything Marc and Bill asked for.

Not long after Tom had hung up the phone with Bill, Chuck called.

"Hello, Tom," he said. "I just wanted to check in and see how things are going. You heard from Bill today, right?"

"Yes." Tom was surprised that Chuck had called so soon after he spoke with Bill. Then a light bulb went off in his head. Bill probably bcc'd Chuck on his e-mails as well. It made sense. Just as John said, the team worked synergistically. That was how they did it.

Chuck asked, "How did it go?"

"I have this paperwork to fill out and documents to assemble. It seems like a lot. There are a lot of questions that seem to have nothing to do with the mortgage, like whether or not I feel that I've saved enough for retirement, if I have enough life insurance, if I have a will, and even what my hobbies are."

"Don't worry," Chuck said. For the first time in days Tom realized he could actually believe those words again. "Just answer the questions the best you can and fill everything out. It's all very important in your overall plan. Marc and I do this for all of our clients and the feedback is incredible. Would you like to see our testimonials book from our clients? There are hundreds of testimonials. I could bring them to our next appointment."

"No, that's okay, Chuck. Kim and I got to look at it in the waiting room at your office. It is very impressive."

Then Tom thought of something else. "Chuck, I know I'm supposed to send Marc a lot of documentation: W-2's, tax returns, and all of my asset statements. The other lender I spoke with didn't ask for this. I'm just curious—why is that? It seems to me the guy didn't know what he was doing."

"I know it's confusing," said Chuck. "Some lenders try to cut corners just to get the business. But it's the client who pays when they do that. If we start with proper documentation, then we can get a real pre-approval. When we have that, we know not only that we are going to get the right mortgage, but we also know for sure that we will be able to close. This is the true advantage of giving Marc a few days to research your options. He can review it with an underwriter, and get a 'real' approval. At that point, he'll be able to see if there are any red flags that need to be addressed now, not when we have an accepted offer and your deposit is on the line.

"One time, I was a buyer's agent on a transaction and my client made an offer on a house with a letter from a lender I did not refer him to. The letter said 'pre-approval,' but it was really only a pre-qualification. Usually pre-qualifications are done from estimates, not real numbers. The offer was accepted and we moved forward past the commitment date only to find later that my buyer could not qualify for a mortgage. But by then it was too late and we had to fight to get the deposit back. Luckily for us, we had a real estate attorney involved."

Tom felt a little nauseous when he thought about his own lost deposit. "Well, I'm definitely not complaining," he said. "I'll give Marc every piece of information he wants and maybe even more."

"Good, but no need to go overboard. Now, would you and Kim be up for a little house hunting on Saturday?"

"You bet."

When the weekend came, Tom and Kim asked John if they could leave the boys with him. The children had a hard enough time understanding the phrase "just looking" in the toy section of a department store. Tom and Kim didn't want to confuse them by looking at houses they might never move into.

Tom was excited. They had already viewed the listings Chuck had sent and felt they were going to see a nice range of homes. They would see houses at both higher and lower price points. They would see ranch-style and two-story homes. They would check out houses in their current school district and homes in a few other neighborhoods.

Tom and Kim found Chuck waiting for them in his office's parking lot. They had decided to ride in his car for the day.

"Let's start a little further out and then we'll work back to your neighborhood. Does that sound good to you?"

Tom and Kim looked at each other, excited, and nodded. "Let's go," said Tom.

By the end of the day, Tom felt his eyes would pop if he had to see one more house, but he and Kim had learned a lot. There were so many things to consider that they hadn't thought about before. Did they want an upstairs? Did they want a house with oil or gas heat? How much lawn was Tom willing to mow all summer? The questions went on and on.

However—and Tom thought this was especially important—they didn't feel overwhelmed or disheartened. Just knowing they had to think about these things made him feel better informed and helped him trust that they would make a good decision. Chuck confirmed this by giving him and Kim a *list*[*] before they went home.

"This is something I give every client after we look at homes," he said. "It's just a few questions you'll want to answer for yourselves, and some things to discuss as a family."

"Wow, this will really help," Tom said. "We already know we have a lot to think about and this will help us focus."

"Yes, thank you so much," Kim said. She took the list from Tom and placed it in the folder Chuck had given them with all the information for the homes they'd seen that day.

---

[*] For a copy of the list go to *www.whats-your-rate.com*

As they drove home, Kim leaned back in her seat and breathed a huge sigh of relief. "I can't believe how much fun that was. It was almost like shopping at the mall."

Tom smiled. He was just happy to hear his wife use the word *fun* again.

At that moment both Tom and Kim's cell phone buzzed. It was an e-mail from Marc's team confirming their meeting the next day, and included an attachment entitled, "What Makes Us Different."

Review

CHAPTER 6

Referral is given to realtor. The best introductions are made via email with both the Realtor and client copied.

CHAPTER 7

Realtor makes appointment at the office.
Buyer meeting at the Realtor's office.
Realtor refers the Mortgage Originator.

CHAPTER 8

Mortgage Originator sets an appointment with the client for a loan consultation.

Pre-consultation worksheets are filled out prior to the consultation and analyzed by the Mortgage Originator.

CHAPTER 9

The Mortgage Originator

The Loan Consultation

"Looking for houses is great, but I'm not looking forward to talking about numbers," Tom said.

"I'm not keen on it either," Kim agreed. "But remember, the hardest time we had with all this was when we didn't understand our numbers and no one would help us with it."

"Yeah," Tom laughed. "I guess this is a case of 'Be careful what you wish for,' huh?"

"I guess so. Let's get going. We don't want to keep Marc waiting."

When they arrived at Marc's office, Tom and Kim were met with the same friendly but professional greeting they had enjoyed at Chuck's office. Someone greeted them, offered them coffee and settled them in the room where Marc would meet with them.

And Marc, just like Chuck, entered very soon after they had poured their coffee. He was tall and athletic and dressed in neatly pressed slacks with a blue shirt and yellow tie. "How are you? I want to thank you so much for the opportunity to work with you."

Tom noticed and liked the fact that Marc used the word *opportunity*. It made him feel as if Marc thought it was a privilege to work with them. He didn't make an assumption as Mr. Becker had.

"I want you to know that my team member, Amy Marie St. James, and I have already been working on loan options and have done some research. We have a good idea of the maximum loan amount you can be pre-approved for, based on your credit score and the up-front documentation you provided. Thank you so much for getting that to us. By the way, you both have excellent credit scores."

"You know, I've always wondered," Tom said. "Can you tell us exactly what's excellent about our scores?"

"I'm glad you asked, Tom," Marc replied. "This is a good time to talk about that. Your credit scores are based on a number of different factors. Your credit score is based on the FICO scoring model. There are three credit bureaus. They are TransUnion, Experian, and Equifax and they each report a score that ranges from 300 to 850. Lenders typically go by the middle score for each borrower, and base the loan evaluation on the lowest score. So for example, Tom, if you have a 700 credit score and Kim has a 660, lenders will underwrite or grade the loan based on the 660. There are different score requirements for various loan programs. Here, this might be easier if I made a visual for you." Marc drew a large circle on a piece of paper and started dividing it into sections. "The score breaks down as such: Thirty-five percent of your score is for payment history, which includes mortgage payments, installment loans, and adverse public records such as bankruptcies, collections, and past dues. Thirty percent of the score is based on amounts owed, which includes the number of accounts, amounts owed on specific accounts, and the proportion of the balanced owed to the total limit or line amount. Fifteen percent is for the length of credit, which consists of the amount of time since an account was opened and the time since there was activity on the account. The longer the account is active, the better it is for the score. This is why it is not advisable to pay off and close out a collection account because you lose the credit for the length of credit history. Ten percent of the score is for the types of credit—mortgage loans and installment loans usually have the largest effect. The last ten percent is for new credit, which consists of the number of recently opened accounts, recent credit inquiries, the amount of time between recent account openings, and the re-establishment of positive credit history.

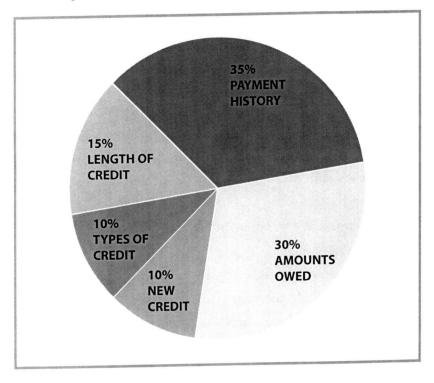

"There are two things that I always want my clients to know with regards to their credit score. Number one, online credit scoring models can be very different from the FICO scoring model that mortgage lenders use, and number two, it is just as easy to damage your credit score as it is to improve it. Like everything else, it needs to be managed."

Again, Tom was pleasantly surprised. He was getting great information—in a way he could understand—and Marc and his team were already working on the loan. This meeting was going to be easier than he had thought. Now he understood why the team did everything up-front as Chuck had said: so they could research all the different programs, and make sure what they chose fit into Tom and Kim's overall financial plan.

"You probably heard this from Bill too, but," Marc said, "I want to congratulate you on selecting Chuck to be your real estate agent. I have been working with Chuck for a long time. He does a fantastic job for all of his clients. How did you meet him?"

"Our neighbor John Randle referred us," Kim said.

"That is a very strong referral. As Chuck may have told you, we only work by referral, and any referral from John is always a quality person. John has given Chuck so many referrals, and they are all such a joy to work with. The old saying is true: birds of a feather flock together."

Tom and Kim looked at each other and beamed. They were "quality" people.

"I don't know if Chuck told you, but I take a different approach from the traditional mortgage originator," Marc said. "I want to make sure that the mortgage you select is integrated into your overall long- and short-term financial and investment goals, as well as your payment, equity, and cash flow objectives."

"There's that phrase again," Tom thought. By now it was like a familiar tune.

"I want to show you how to use this mortgage loan as a financial instrument in your overall financial plan. I will help you manage it with either your financial advisor or a financial advisor I recommend," said Marc. "Is that okay and does that make sense?"

"Yes, absolutely," said Tom.

"Now, before we discuss loan scenarios," said Marc, "I want to ask you about your financial team. The questions regarding your relationships with those team members were left blank on the *Mortgage Planning Analysis form,*" so I'd like to review them with you."

Tom and Kim nodded in agreement.

"Have you considered how this mortgage will fit into your retirement, your protection needs, potential college investment, or any other goals you may have?"

"No," Tom admitted. "I think our main concern was that the house wouldn't block us down the line when we wanted to do those things. I actually thought we would purchase the home, and address the rest when there was a need."

"Well, Tom, a lot of people think that way," said Marc. "But if you want to achieve your goals it is very important to have a team set up as soon as possible."

"Yes, John told me all about it. He kept telling me how important it was to stay on course with my team."

"He's absolutely right," said Marc. "Most people start building a team, but they stop part way. They think, just as you have, that they would do the rest when the time came and a need presented itself. But if I told you it would be relatively easy, wouldn't it make sense to do it now? One of the biggest problems I see today is that people compartmentalize their financial decisions and put off what is not an immediate concern. But every financial decision you make has an effect on your overall financial plan. You must integrate them all together."

---

* For a copy of the Mortgage Planning Analysis form go to *www.whats-your-rate.com*

Kim said, "We really don't have much money to invest right now."

"Sometimes there are more important things to consider than just investing," said Marc. "How is your relationship with your financial advisor who specializes in insurance protection, retirement planning, and investments?"

"We don't have a financial advisor yet," Tom said. "But I know we're supposed to have one as part of the team of advisors."

"Good, I'm glad we're on the same page. Now, how is your relationship with your accountant?"

"Up until now we haven't had one," Kim said. "We've been doing our own taxes using TurboTax."

Marc nodded. "When you do purchase your home, you will have some tax benefits that you will need a professional to help you with. The financial advisor that I refer you to will recommend the accountant on our team to help you. You could get started right away. It may be a good idea to adjust your W-4 withholding at work and increase your deductions, so that you get your tax money in your paycheck instead of having to wait until the end of the year for a big refund. I would rather see you have use of the money, instead of letting the government earn interest on it for a year before they distribute it as a tax refund."

Tom was amazed. He never thought he could have any say over how he paid his taxes or how much of a refund he received.

"How is your relationship with your estate planning attorney?" Marc asked.

Tom sighed and thought of his nightmare again. "We don't have one."

"That's not surprising when you consider that more than half of the people in America don't have a will. Without a will in place when you die, the government will make all the decisions for you regarding your estate and your children. The estate has to go through probate court, which can be very expensive and time consuming, and not something you would want to put your loved ones through when they are grieving."

"You'll get no argument here," Tom said. "I know how important it is to take care of my family. We are open to moving forward with what is best for us as soon as possible."

"Good. The financial advisor that you speak with will introduce you to the estate planning attorney as well. Now, getting back to your team, how is your relationship with your insurance professional who specializes in the homeowner's insurance?"

"We don't have one yet," Tom said, "but we figured we would just call the agent who handles our car insurance."

"That's what most people do," Marc said, "but I would prefer that you review all of your insurance needs together. We have an expert who we always recommend. He will make sure that he also discusses an umbrella policy as well as your basic homeowner's insurance. I will send you a reminder regarding the insurance binder you will need, along with the agent's contact information. Do you know what an umbrella policy is?"

Tom and Kim shook their heads.

"I find that most people don't," said Mark.

"An umbrella policy basically covers all other aspects of your financial life. There are many unexpected events that people never think of that could ruin them financially. One of my clients was a very famous former athlete. I was a big fan of his for many years. One day, he was referred to me for a mortgage. I was excited to be working with a celebrity and was curious how much money he had accumulated from all those years in professional sports.

"When he came into my office, he looked as if he had the weight of the world on his shoulders. We reviewed his situation, and it turned out he had lost most of his assets. He had gone through a bankruptcy and a nervous breakdown. I found out he had been a car accident, in which he was at fault, and the other person was very badly injured. He lost all of his personal wealth in the lawsuit and had to file bankruptcy because the damage was more than his homeowner's insurance covered. Here's an interesting statistic: 1 in every 1,200 houses burn down, yet every mortgage loan requires fire insurance. However, 1 in every 200 people get sued in their lifetime, but the vast majority don't have an umbrella policy in place. It makes very little sense.

"If this athlete client had an umbrella policy, which is not expensive at all, he would have been covered and his assets would have been protected. That one hole in his financial plan cost him everything that he had worked for. You see, dealing with your finances is like keeping a car in alignment. If one wheel is not in balance with the others, eventually that one wheel can ruin the rest. The more assets you have, the more complicated the financial plan."

This surprised Tom. "I guess even a rich person, who seems to have everything under control, can be wiped out if one part of the puzzle is missing." "Yes," Marc said. "It goes to show that even the wealthy need to stay on top of their finances. In fact, I'd go so far as to say the reason the wealthy are wealthy is because they constantly monitor the details of their money.

"Your Core 7 team will help you do that. When buying a home, most people only work with a realtor, a loan originator, a property and casualty insurance agent, and a real estate attorney because those are the people they need to purchase a home. I encourage my clients to go the distance and get the final three: a financial advisor to manage their assets, investments, and protection needs, an accountant to maximize cash flow, tax incentives, and deductions, and an estate planning attorney to make sure their wealth and dreams are passed down properly to the next generation."

Tom nodded. "John stressed this with me as well, but you've made it crystal clear now why we need the whole team. Thank you for that."

"It is my pleasure. During this process we will make sure you have your whole financial picture covered. Now that we've discussed your team and some of your goals, let's talk about your mortgage. Help me understand, what's most important about this home loan to you?"

"To be able to make the payments comfortably, so that my family is secure." Tom looked at Kim for confirmation. She nodded.

"Help me understand," Marc went on, "what would make you feel that your family is secure?"

Tom remembered his nightmare and shuddered. "To know that if anything bad happened, for example, if I got injured on the job, or died suddenly, or anything," Tom paused. "I'd like to know that my family would be okay and financially stable without me, and not have the burden of the mortgage."

"And of course we also want to be able to save enough money to send our children to college," Kim said, "and also save enough to retire comfortably."

"And still leave something behind," Tom added. "I'd really like to be able to purchase a second home some day, maybe buy some real estate for investment purposes and build a real estate portfolio. You know, something that would continue to gain value for my children. We have already spoken with Chuck about this and have a goal to buy investment property in the near future."

Marc listened intently and, Tom noticed, took a lot of notes. "Thank you for letting me know that, and for sharing all of the things that are important to you. Typically, most clients don't think that far ahead."

"Chuck really helped us paint a picture of what we wanted our future to look like beyond the purchase of this home," Tom said.

"I think that we'll be able to cover all of what you want to do and make you feel comfortable with our process," Marc said. "Now let's discuss the specifics of the loan. Okay?"

"That's fine. Let's do it," said Tom.

"A good place to start would be with the down payment and what you qualify for. I know your intention is to put 10 percent down, which would be most of your savings, but I would also like to show you a scenario where you only put 3.5 percent down. It may make sense to put less money down and keep the rest in a reserve account. This is something you will want to discuss with the financial advisor, but I wanted to make the option available to you in case he makes that suggestion. I have a feeling that cash reserves are going to be a priority.

"My goal is for you to be pre-approved in the next couple days so that you will be able to make an offer on a property. This will be a real pre-approval because you have gotten us all of your paperwork, which we will run through our underwriting system. This will make your offer much stronger than someone who only has a pre-quali-fication, which means their lender has not analyzed and verified if everything on their loan application is accurate.

"Just for your own information, the way I determine the loan amount that you qualify for is the same way that any lender would do it. It's based on debt to income ratios."

Tom sat up—the mysterious ratios. "I've been curious to know what that all meant."

"No problem. It's fairly easy to explain. First, there's something I want you to understand—there are many different ratios for various products and loan scenarios. For the loan program that I feel is the best fit for you, the ratios are 31 percent/43 percent. These are just guidelines. Lenders may allow you to go much higher with compensating factors like strong credit, a lot of cash reserves, and large down payments. Each loan is unique, and ultimately everything comes down to the underwriter's discretion. Here is what these numbers mean: the first number, in this case, 31 percent, is called your front-end ratio. It's a percentage of your gross monthly income, which represents your total housing expense and includes principal, interest, taxes, and insurance or condominium fees, and private mortgage insurance, if applicable. The second number, in this case 43 percent, is called your back-end ratio. It is also a percentage of your gross monthly income, but it includes your total housing expense plus your monthly revolving and installment debt. This could also include things like alimony, child support, loans you've co-signed for, and 401k loans. For example, using the 31 percent/43 percent ratio, if your gross monthly income were $10,000 per month, your front-end ratio would be $3,100 a month and your back-end ratio would be $4,300.

"What I do for my clients is have them meet with the financial advisor on my team to do a full *cash flow analysis*.* This will factor in what you spend on entertainment, what you spend on your children, and other debt that a mortgage will not cover. Lenders aren't taking into account if you go out to eat three times a week to nice restau-

---

* For a copy of the cash flow analysis go to *www.whats-your-rate.com*

rants, have a child in daycare, a nanny, or an addiction to Jimmy Choo shoes."

Kim giggled at the shoe reference.

INCOME	=	$120,000/yr	÷	12 months	=	MONTHLY INCOME *of* $10,000
MAXIMUM MONTHLY MORTAGE PAYMENT (principal, interest, taxes, mortgage insurance, homeowners insurance, condominium fees)	=	31% (housing ratio)	*of*	$10,000 (gross monthly income)	=	$3,100
MAXIMUM MONTHLY DEBT (Total mortgage payments and installment debt, credit card debt payments, 401k loan payments, rental losses on investment property)	=	43% (total debt ratio)	*of*	$10,000 (gross monthly income)	=	$4,300

"Lenders don't factor this in, but you obviously should," Marc went on. "The lending powers that exist assume that you'll give up your luxuries if the choice is between the luxuries and your home, and they are probably right, but do you really want to give up your luxuries? I find working with a professional to sort through these questions is time well spent. As we discussed, I am going to have the financial advisor on my team get in touch with you. Okay?"

"That would be great." Tom said. "This was our biggest issue from the beginning. We weren't sure how the payments would fit in with our overall financial picture, and no one seemed interested in helping us figure it out. I'm really seeing the importance of having a team in place—I feel we're getting all the help we need to get our questions answered."

"That's certainly what we're here for. Okay, let me ask you, how long do you plan on being in this loan?"

Tom and Kim looked at each other. "Loan?" Kim asked. "You mean how long will we be in the house, right?"

"We were thinking that we'd live in whatever house we choose forever," Tom said. "So we should look into a 30-year fixed loan, right? This other guy that Gwendolyn Davis had us speak to suggested that we do an adjustable rate mortgage. It sounds like a terrible loan. Why would anyone ever do that?"

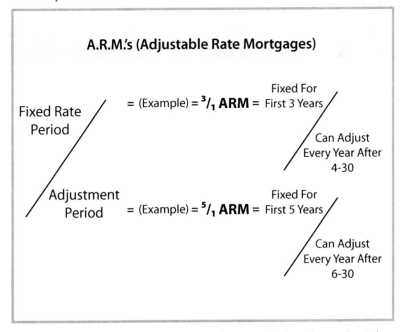

Marc folded his hands on the table. "Well, that depends. Adjustable rate loans typically have a lower interest rate for the initial fixed period. For example, if you choose a 5/1 ARM, the interest rate is fixed for five years. If you choose a 7/1 ARM, it's fixed for seven years, and so on. Even though you feel that you are going to live in this home for the rest of your life, that does not necessarily mean a 30-year fixed loan is the proper structure. There are many other things to think of. Maybe you will be doing some significant construction to this home? You might want to add another bedroom as your family grows?"

"Well, it's funny you say that—we are expecting another child," said Tom.

"Congratulations! That's important to know. So if, for instance, you purchased a home with three bedrooms and you knew that you may need to add a fourth, you may want to look at an adjustable rate mortgage that is fixed for a shorter period of time with a lower payment. If you were going to do a 30-year fixed mortgage, but after five years needed to do a $100,000 addition, my question to you would be, where are you going to get the money for the construction?"

Example using $200,000 loan 30 year fixed at 5% $^5/_1$ ARM at 4%						
Fixed Rate Loan	1	2	3	4	5	6
	5%	5%	5%	5%	5%	(Need $100,000 for the construction. Need to refinance for $300,000)
	$1073.64	$1073.64	$1073.64	$1073.64	$1073.64	
	Total Payment = $5,368.21 (principal & interest)					
ARM Adjustable Rate Mortgage	1	2	3	4	5	6
	4%	4%	4%	4%	4%	(Need $100,000 for the construction. Need to refinance for $300,000.) So you never hit the "adjustment period" of the ARM.
	$954.83	$954.83	$954.83	$954.83	$954.83	
	Total Payment = $4,774.15 (principal & interest)					
Savings Difference = $594.21/yr Savings Difference over 5 yrs = $2971.08						
*does not include taxes						

"I don't know," Tom admitted.

"You would probably have to get a construction loan, which is basically a refinance, to replace the loan we are discussing now. So locking in a loan that's fixed for thirty years would not be the best financial decision in that scenario. You would only be in the loan that we used to purchase this home for five years, and then have to restructure it to finance the addition of the fourth bedroom. Does that make sense?"

Tom and Kim nodded, listening intently.

"There are other reasons people look at ARMs. Some people are more aggressive in their investments and believe they can get a better return on the savings between the fixed rate payment and the adjustable rate payment. Maybe they invest it somewhere else, where the savings can earn a higher return. As I mentioned earlier, adjustable rate mortgages typically have a lower interest rate. Let me show you how this would work based on a $300,000, 30-year fixed loan at a 5 percent interest rate. The principal and interest payment would be $1,610 per month. Compare that to a $300,000, 5/1 ARM at a 4 percent interest rate. The principal and interest payment on that loan would be $1,432 a month. That's a $177 difference. You could allocate that additional $177 elsewhere where it could earn a better rate of return. This strategy is called arbitrage. People in favor of this strategy also like the fact that the $177 is more accessible. They can access the money whenever it is needed.

"Although many are successful with this method, there is risk involved. It requires a lot of involvement, and you need to feel comfortable with potential rate changes and volatility. Most people like the 30-year fixed mortgage because it helps them sleep better at night, and if this is your case, I think it's the right option. Think of the slightly higher payment with the 30-year fixed loan as an insurance policy that ensures that your rate and payment will never change. Does that make sense?"

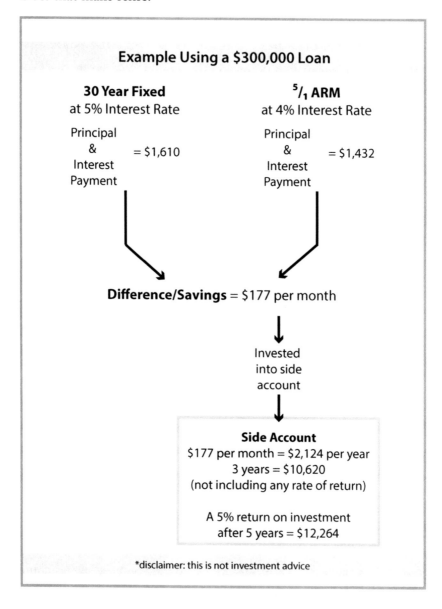

Example Using a $300,000 Loan

30 Year Fixed
at 5% Interest Rate

Principal & Interest Payment = $1,610

⁵/₁ ARM
at 4% Interest Rate

Principal & Interest Payment = $1,432

Difference/Savings = $177 per month

Invested into side account

Side Account
$177 per month = $2,124 per year
3 years = $10,620
(not including any rate of return)

A 5% return on investment
after 5 years = $12,264

*disclaimer: this is not investment advice

"Yeah, it really does." Tom was impressed and relieved. Marc obviously knew his stuff. "Thank you for the information. But I can tell you that Chuck is looking for a four-bedroom house that we are hoping will be everything we are asking for. I think we'd feel more comfortable with a 30-year fixed mortgage because we want to make sure that the rate cannot change. We like to plan ahead and know what we are doing with our money. We don't want to be concerned or worried about any potential risk." Kim nodded in agreement.

"That's great," Marc said. "I'm glad I asked the question. The reason I always make sure to touch on things my clients may not necessarily be thinking about, like the features of ARMs, is to ensure you clearly understand all of the options. I was pretty sure you were more comfortable with the 30-year fixed loan, but I always like to address everything you may hear about. My biggest fear is that after your loan closes and you are in your home, you may be speaking with a friend or co-worker and hear about something we did not discuss, and say, 'Why didn't Marc tell us about that?' That is why I always address any and all aspects that may come up in the conversation.

"I know we're touching on a lot of details, so I should mention that at this point we're just in the pre-approval process. We can make adjustments once you find the property. You are not obligated to decide on the exact structure today. Pre-approval is to find out how much you can qualify for, explain the process, answer any questions you have, and advise you on your options. You are not bound by your pre-approval. Now the paperwork we need to review for your loan should be ready. I'll just go get it." Marc got up and left the room. Tom and Kim looked at each other and sighed.

"This isn't so bad," Kim said. She got up to get the coffee pot to refill their coffees. Tom noticed a concerned look on Kim's face and asked, "Everything okay?"

"Yes", Kim said, "but when Marc was talking about life insurance and wills, it really scared me. I don't know what I would do if something happened to you. What would the kids do if something happened to either of us?"

"I feel I've already lived it." Tom told Kim about his nightmare.

"Honey, that's terrible. Why didn't you tell me about it before?"

"I don't know. Maybe that would have made it too real and there was nothing I could do about it. Maybe I can talk about it now because Marc has shown me there's a lot we can do."

"Yes, and we're still young enough to do it. I was feeling bad because we didn't have all the advisors Marc was talking about. But now I see how we're going to get it together and they're going to help us. All the questions about the team were helpful too. But I wonder what would happen if we already had some of those people in place, like an accountant?"

"Why don't we just ask Marc? I was curious about that too."

"Okay." Marc returned and took his seat at the table with some papers in hand.

"Hey, Marc, I know this has nothing to do with our loan, but Kim and I were just curious. What do you do if a new client of yours already has some of these professionals in place?"

Marc nodded. "That is a great question, Tom. If they have someone in place, let's say a financial advisor, an accountant, or an estate planner, I ask the client's permission to contact him or her. Then, I can discuss how we are structuring the loan and introduce the other members of our team. The key is that the customer has their whole Core 7 financial team in place.

"To be honest, it works great because my partners love it. They get the opportunity to meet other business sources. One of my clients may have a great accountant, but not have a financial advisor. I will introduce my financial advisor to the client, and also to the client's accountant. Everyone gets to make new connections and that's important in our work."

Marc then handed Tom and Kim papers titled total cost analysis. "Here's the information on your loan showing the 10 percent down we discussed and the 3.5 percent down. I've made this spreadsheet so it'll be easier for you to understand everything. I find visuals really help.

3.5% vs. 10% Down

SUMMARY

1st MTG.	Program Name	3.5% Down	10% Down
	Loan Amount	$300,000	$279,792
	Interest Rate	4.5 %	4.5 %
	Term (months)	360	360
	Payment	$1,520	$1,418
	Mtg. Ins.	$0	$0
	Monthy Payment	$1,502	$1,418
	Tax Benefits	$394	$367
	After Tax Payment	$1,126	$1,050
	Net Savings	$0	**$76**

TOTAL COST ANALYSIS

360 MONTHS ANALYSIS	Program Name	3.5% Down	10% Down
	Total Payment	$547,220	$510,359
	Principal Paid	$300,000	$279,792
	Int & MI Paid	$247,220	$230,567
	Balance Left	$0	$0
	Closing & Points	$0	$0
	Total Cost	$247,220	$230,567
	Tax Benefits	$86,527	$80,699
	After Tax Cost	$160,693	$149,869
	Net Savings	$0	**$10,824**

"The loan amounts here are based on ratios that I feel are best for you to comfortably make your mortgage payment while also being able to invest in your other goals. It's important that you have the money to enjoy your life and not feel you are living to pay your mortgage. You could qualify for more, but I used these numbers because I believe they are ideal, based on everything we discussed. Does that make sense?"

"Yes. Kim and I want to have something left over for our other goals."

"In this first part, you'll see an illustration of exactly what you'll be making for a monthly payment and the exact tax benefit that you would be receiving. Now in the next section, you'll see how much you would be paying over the next thirty years. As you can see, over the next thirty years, your $300,000 mortgage will cost you almost $600,000 in principal and interest."

"Wow! That's a lot of money for a $300,000 loan," Kim said.

"Yes it is," Marc said. "However, since you plan on being employed for those thirty years, the tax benefit you receive from home ownership will help you offset a good amount of it. This is how the government incentivizes homebuyers.

"I'm sure the financial advisor I'm going to refer you to will show you ways to free up money by increasing your tax savings, or cutting back on your spending on expenses such as your phone bill, cable bill, dining out, and many other things. The most important thing to finding savings or freeing up monthly cash flow is not to spend the money. Once you free up the cash, make sure you start contributing it to your investments. Your financial planner can set it up so this comes out of your bank account automatically so you never actually notice the money."

Tom thought that was a great idea. He nodded his approval as he took another look at the total cost analysis. He noticed another set of figures. "Now, Marc, are these the interest rates we will be getting?"

"Great question, Tom," Marc replied. "This is a good time to discuss interest rates. First let me ask you: do you know where mortgage rates come from and how they are set?"

"No, we just know we were supposed to ask about the rates. That was one of the things we were very confused about when we spoke to the other lender."

"Mortgage rates are based on the secondary bond market on Wall Street. Rates change multiple times a day, in a similar manner to stock prices. In the past, banks adjusted their rates once a week because there was no secondary bond market. The bank that was lending the money actually held the mortgage, which was funded from deposits from bank customers. But the creation of the secondary market is a great thing because it keeps liquidity in the market so that banks can keep lending and make homeownership possible for more people.

"There are many different economic events that happen during the day that can affect interest rates. For example, reports on inflation, employment figures, political unrest and terrorism, natural disasters, changes in the stock market, and many other factors. With these events happening so frequently, and many times unexpectedly, it is nearly impossible to just show the lowest interest rate because they are constantly changing.

"To simplify this even further, think about this. Good news about the economy is generally bad news for mortgage rates. Bad news about the economy is unfortunately good news for interest rates. When 9/11 happened, interest rates plummeted. On the flip side, when we get better-than-expected results on, say, the job market, which is good news about the economy, interest rates rise."

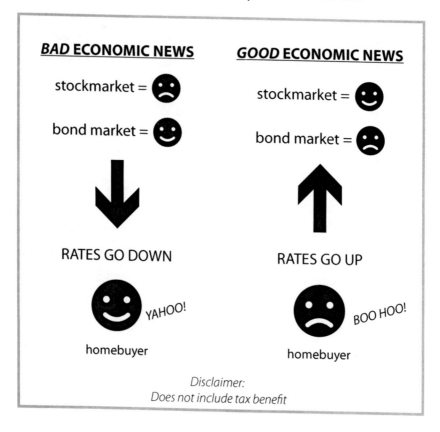

"Okay, I'm beginning to understand this now," Tom said. "So if I were shopping around—not that we would want to—Kim and I are really comfortable with you—but if we were still looking, how do I know that I am getting the best interest rate? If I walked out of here today and saw an ad offering a lower rate, how would I find comparisons? By looking online?"

"It is good to look online to get an idea of where rates are and the range that they are traveling," Marc said. "However, there are many rate and fee combinations to consider, and many times online rates are not accurate. They could be as much as a week old. Rates typically travel in a tight range on a daily basis.

"The market is constantly moving. You could be looking at a rate online that could change five minutes later because of something that happened in the bond market. Many things such as a positive unemployment report, a positive retail sales figure, the stock market rallying, or a terrorist threat could change the interest rate market."

"Wow, I didn't know it could happen that fast," Tom said.

"Yes, and now you begin to see the issue," Marc added. "A real estate deal doesn't happen quickly. First, mortgage interest rates change daily, based on the mortgage backed securities market. If you are closing forty-five days from now, there is a chance that rates will change many times or stay the same depending on the market. Second, if my company prices a loan at 9 a.m. eastern time, and another mortgage company prices their rates today at 10 a.m. eastern time, there is a chance that one of us could be .125 percent higher or lower than the other. This is why it can be confusing when comparing lenders by rate alone—it is a never-ending cycle. This is why I built my mortgage practice around making sure the loan is integrated into someone's overall financial plan and measured over time.

"What's interesting is that so many people will shop around and choose one lender over another based on that .125 percent. Do you know how much they save when they do that?"

Tom and Kim shook their heads.

"It's less than $3 a week, after tax, for every .125 percent on a $300,000 loan. That's less than a large caramel macchiato gourmet coffee. I don't know about you, but my wife gets a large caramel macchiato every day. That's .750 percent in interest rate."

The Cost Of .125%

$300,000
5%

$300,000
4.875%

Principal
&
Interest
= $1,610

Principal
&
Interest
= $1,588

$22 per month
savings

$12 per month
savings after taxes

=$2.77 per week

1 less coffee per week? = $2.95 per week

sun	mon	tues	wed	thurs	fri	sat

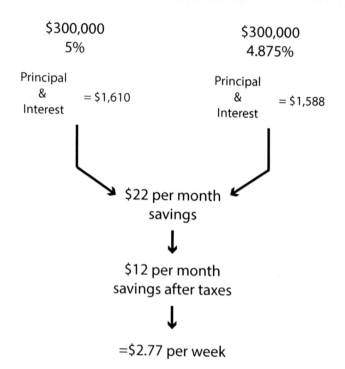

OR

Switch from a Large to a Medium? = $3.50 per week

Large Starbucks Coffee = $2.95

Medium Starbucks Coffee = $2.45

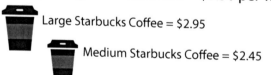

There are better places to save!

"Sounds like someone I know," Tom said, nudging Kim in the side. As they all laughed, Tom thought again of how much he was enjoying the conversation.

"For a clearer example," Marc said, "let's say you are in the 35 percent tax bracket, borrowing $300,000 at a rate of 5 percent. Your principal and interest payment is $1,610. At 4.875 percent, your payment is $1,588 for a savings of $22 per month and $276 per year. However, after taxes it is only about $12 per month and $144 per year. That's $2.77 per week. You could save that by going one day without a coffee.

"Look, I know you're working on assembling your Core 7," Marc said. "Paying all these professionals is obviously going to be a consideration. The point I'm making here is that while there are costs involved to work with these advisors—who will give you valuable advice on your mortgage, your financial insurance needs, passing your assets down to loved ones, buying a home, and protecting yourself in all areas—these costs can be offset in a number of ways. Often you can save the same amount of money by just going from a large coffee to a medium coffee, packing lunch a few times a week instead of ordering out, or renting a DVD instead of going to a movie theater. Your advisors are much too valuable, and should be the last thing that you choose based on price alone."

Marc added, "Now don't get me wrong. Price is important, and should be competitive. As it applies to your mortgage, I have an unwritten policy in place called the .125 percent policy. What that means to you is that we want you to look around and compare the different prices out there. And if on the same day at the same time, with an apples-to-apples comparison, we cannot match, beat, or at least come within .125 percent, we will help you get all your paperwork over to the mortgage consultant of your choosing, and still remain a resource for you, and a trusted adviser throughout the whole process. Is that fair?"

"More than fair. Look, Kim and I think your team is very professional and you've been giving us great advice. Quite frankly, we're not even going to call anyone else because I see now that the advice from you and your team is far more valuable than .125 percent."

Tom didn't say it, but he was also very happy that Marc had fully addressed the price issue. He thought it showed a lot of confidence on Marc's part, and that he cared for them to not only get great service, but to also get a competitive price. But there was one thing he was still curious about and wanted to ask.

"Marc, we received your e-mail attachment this morning. Could you clarify the details of what makes you different from the other loan officers?"

Marc smiled. "That's a great question and I'm glad you asked. There are a couple reasons. First of all, as I said earlier, I don't see myself in the business of just selling you a loan. I see my primary goal as helping you integrate the mortgage into your long- and short-term financial investment goals and your payment, equity, and cash flow objectives, helping create wealth for you and your family.

"And the second reason is I see my job continuing even after the loan closes—I want to be a resource to you. So we stay in touch and monitor your interest rates and loan structure. I make sure that you always have the lowest cost mortgage the market has to offer. I also want to be the point person with your other advisors collaborating on your best interests.

"Let me give you an example of what I mean." Marc took a printed report out of a folder and passed it to Tom and Kim. "I send out this report quarterly." It shows you the exact balance of your loan and how your loan compares to the current market. And even if the interest rate is higher than the one you currently have, at least you'll know that the structure of your current loan is best."

Rate Watch Analysis

CURRENT LOAN

Start Date	Lien Position	Loan Balance	Rate	Term	→ Current Payment:
June 2004	1st	$307,653	5.250%	21.92 yrs	$1,971

MONTHLY HIGHLIGHTED PROGRAM

Program	Int. Rate	APR	Term	→ Recommended Payment:
30 Year Fixed	3.750%	3.835%	30 yrs	$1,425

$547
Payment Difference

CURRENT MARKET PROGRAMS

Program Name	Int. Rate	Term	Current Payment	Proposed Payment	Monthly Difference	APR
30 YEAR FIXED	3.750%	30 yrs	$1,971	$1,125	$517 Decrease	3.835%
5/1 ARM	3.125%	30 yrs	$1,971	$1,318	$653 Decrease	3.207%
7/1 ARM	3.375%	30 yrs	$1,971	$1,360	$611 Decrease	3.458%
20 YEAR FIXED	3.625%	20 yrs	$1,971	$1,804	$167 Decrease	3.743%
15 YEAR FIXED	3.250%	15 yrs	$1,971	$2,162	$190 Decrease	3.400%

FREEDOM POINT REMINDER WITH TERM REDUCTION STRATEGY

Investment Strategy

Monthly Pre-Pay Amount	Total Interest Savings	Freedom Point
$100	$20,604	20.08 Years
$200	$37,355	18.50 Years
$300	$51,273	17.17 Years

NOTES & SPECIAL ANNOUNCEMENTS

This Ratewatch report is designed to give you an overview of how your mortgage is performing based on the current market. It may, or may not, make sense to refinance based on today's rates. The intent of my monthly Ratewatch service is to keep you informed. If there are any questions you have pertaining to the information contained in this update, please call or contact me. (Rates above are based on single family Owner Occupied Properties with a 60 day rate lock. Please contact me to review your individual situation.)

Tom was surprised. "So after we close, you're telling me if the rate drops, it might make sense to refinance? And you will contact me? Can you tell me how that works? Will I have to pay all those closing costs again?"

"Yes, I will definitely contact you," Marc replied. "I'd much rather help my clients who trust me by staying in touch with them consistently. So hopefully you'll feel good about telling your friends and family about us. And for the refinance, we can do a no-points, no-closing-cost refinance where the lender pays all of your fees."

"That's awesome, but how are there no closing costs? How does anyone make any money?"

"That's a great question and a very common one," Marc replied. "There are always closing costs, but we are receiving enough revenue from the secondary market to be profitable for the lender and pay your closing costs. So, for example, if you were looking in the newspaper today, you may see 4.5 percent as an interest rate. That rate would have closing costs, but at 4.75 percent, the secondary market will give us enough to also pay your closing costs on refinance loans. Many lenders add these closing costs to the end of the loan. In that instance, you would be paying interest on the rolled-in closing costs for thirty years, and that may not be the most cost effective strategy. Even though the interest rate would be lower, paying the closing costs would actually take much longer to recoup and could be more expensive. I'll be able to monitor that for you."

"I like the sound of that," Kim said. "But can we cross that bridge when we come to it? I'd rather focus on this loan right now."

"Yeah, you're right," Tom said, "or else my head will explode with all this new information."

"That's fine. I don't want to overwhelm you," Marc agreed.

No Points/No Closing Vs. Paying Closing Costs

$300,000 Loan

No Points/No Closing

4.75

| Principal
&
Interest | = $1,565 |

300,000 Loan

4.5

| Principal
&
Interest | = $1,520 |

savings = $45

$45 ÷ $3,000 = 66.66 months or 5.5 years
(estimate)   breakeven point

If It Is a Refinance

No Points/No Closing

4.75

$300,000

| Principal
&
Interest | = $1,565 |

With Closing Rolled In

4.5

$303,000

| Principal
&
Interest | = $1,535 |

savings = $30.00 per month

$30 ÷ $3,000 = 100 months or 8.33 years to break even

does not include tax benefit

"Now, since we are looking at a 30-year fixed, and I see from your Mortgage Planning Analysis form that having the lowest interest rate at the lowest payment possible is very important to you. Have you considered paying points to lower the rate? Points are fully tax-deductible in the first year on a purchase, and will lower your rate and payment. As a side note, if you were paying points on a refinance, the tax savings would be amortized or spread out over the life of the loan."

$100,000 Loan Amount

1 point = 1% of Loan amount = 1% of $100,000 = $1,000

3 points = 3% of Loan amount = 3% of $100,000 = $3,000

SUMMARY

1st MTG.	Program Name	0 points	1 point	2 points	3 points
	Loan Amount	$100,000	$100,000	$100,000	$100,000
	Interest Rate	4.5 %	4.25 %	4 %	3.75 %
	Term (months)	360	360	360	360
	Payment	$507	$492	$477	$463
	Mtg. Ins.	$0	$0	$0	$0
	Monthy Payment	$507	$492	$477	$463
	Net Savings	$0	$15	$29	$44

TOTAL COST ANALYSIS

96 MONTHS ANALYSIS	Program Name	0 points	1 point	2 points	3 points
	Total Payment	$48,642	$47,226	$45,832	$44,459
	Principal Paid	$15,183	$15,720	$16,270	$16,832
	Int & MI Paid	$33,459	$31,506	$29,562	$27,627
	Balance Left	$84,817	$84,280	$83,730	$83,168
	Closing & Points	$3,000	$4,000	$5,000	$6,000
	Total Cost	$36,459	$35,506	$34,562	$33,627
	Net Savings	$0	$953	$1,896	$2,831

"Well, we really don't know what points are. I've only heard that we should never pay for points. Could you please explain how they work?"

"Of course, no problem." Marc took out of sheet of paper. "The definition of a point is 1 percent of the loan amount. So for example, if you were taking a $100,000 loan, the cost of one point would be $1,000, and 3 points would be $3,000." He wrote the numbers on the paper as he spoke them. "You can pay points to lower the interest rate. Each point would generally lower the rate between .250 percent and .375 percent. The way to figure out if it makes sense to pay points is to take the monthly savings from the lower interest rate and divide it into the cost of a point(s) to find your breakeven point. Let's use that $100,000 loan at 5 percent as an example. The payment is $536 per month. By buying one point for $1,000, the rate would drop to 4.75, giving you a payment of $521 per month. So we would take the $15 per month savings and divide it into the $1,000 you paid for the point. It would take roughly sixty-seven months, or 5.7 years, to recoup the cost of the point. That is your break-even point. After the 5.7 years, you would save $15 per month for the remaining time you have this loan.

"Has Chuck explained what a seller concession is yet?"

"Yes, briefly, but not in any detail," said Tom.

"That's okay. The idea is that any points and closing costs can be rolled into the loan in the form of what is called a seller concession. This could provide you with the ability to keep more money liquid upfront and also give you some extra money as a reserve account or emergency account."

"Extra money? Is that really possible?"

"We could use that money to buy furniture for the new house," Kim said. "That would be so great."

"Yes, as long as you don't finance the purchase of the furniture before your loan closes," said Marc, "because it could affect your loan approval and you would have to document any credit inquiries to show you have not taken on any new debt. It is explained in the copy of the 'Do's and Don'ts When Applying for a Mortgage'' flyer that Bill sent you. Chuck will explain the seller concession in much more detail to see if it makes sense for you.

"Now I quickly want to address closing costs. The required costs, optional costs, and the monies that you bring to closing can be confusing. I am going to estimate, so you can get a good idea of the total fees and monies needed. This will be disclosed in your good faith estimate when your loan goes into process. The required closing costs will be in the $2,500–$3,500 dollar range, depending on the amount you finance. This includes lender fees, attorney fees, and lender's title insurance, which is typically $2.50 per $1,000 borrowed. The optional costs are the attorney's buyer representation fee, which typically ranges from $500–$1,000, and the owner's title insurance.

"Attorneys will typically give a discount if they are also representing the buyer and the lender and can bundle the lenders and owner's title insurance. Lender's title insurance is required on all loans and protects the lender. The owner's title is optional and protects you. It is roughly $1.50 per thousand dollars of money borrowed. I highly recommend purchasing owner's title insurance and obtaining the buyer representation. Josh Rodman, the attorney that Chuck will recommend, will be able to give you a better explanation of why you should purchase owner's title insurance. Be sure to ask him about it.

---

* For a copy of the "Do's and Don'ts When Applying for a Mortgage" flyer go to *www.whats-your-rate.com*

"Next is establishing your escrow account. These are not actual 'fees,' but monies you will need to bring to closing. They will be put in an escrow account earmarked to pay for your taxes, homeowner's insurance, PMI if applicable, and any per diem interest you may have at the time of closing. In some cases, you can waive the need for your escrow account, but it can result in slightly higher closing costs or a slightly higher interest rate."

"Per diem interest? What's that?" asked Tom.

"Interest is calculated on a daily basis," Marc explained. "So for example, if you close on the fifteenth of the month, the lender would require you to bring fifteen days of interest to closing. If you borrowed $300,000 at 5 percent, your per diem interest would be $41.09 per day, so you would need to put $615.55, $41.09 over 15 days, into your escrow account."

Pre-Paid Interest

$300,000 at 5% Interest Rate = $41.09 per diem interest per day
$300,000 x .005 ÷ 365 = 41.09

If you are closing on the 15th of the month, therefore 15 days of prepaid interest need to be collected. = 15 x 41.09 = $615.55 to be held in your escrow account

---

"Okay, I see. Anything else?"

"You should expect to bring four months of taxes, two months of homeowner's insurance, and be ready to pay for a year of homeowner's insurance in advance. If you have PMI, lenders will usually want one to two months held in escrow also. Now, you should receive your pre-approval via e-mail in the next day or so. Would it be okay if I included Chuck on this so he will also have a copy?"

"Of course," Tom replied. "We're meeting with him on Saturday and we're very excited to look at homes, especially now that we know so clearly what we can afford. Marc, thank you."

"What I'd like to do now is make the introduction to Michael Conroy, the financial advisor on my team. With your permission, I'm going to e-mail some of the documentation you provided, along with the total cost analysis we went over. This will assist him in preparing for your meeting and for a cash flow analysis."

"Absolutely," Tom said.

Kim and Tom really felt comfortable. They couldn't help marveling over the extra service, and how much better they were being treated. John was definitely right. Tom would check in with John when they got home to tell him so. He laughed to himself. He needed to cut down on those expensive coffees, and start drinking it at home. If he saved that money, it could be college tuition in a few years.

Review

CHAPTER 6

Referral is given to Realtor. The best introductions are made via email with both the Realtor and client copied.

CHAPTER 7

Realtor makes appointment at the office.
Buyer meeting at the Realtor's office.
Realtor refers the Mortgage Originator.

CHAPTER 8

Mortgage Originator sets an appointment with the client for a loan consultation. Pre-consultation worksheets are filled out prior to the consultation and analyzed by the Mortgage Originator.

CHAPTER 9

The Loan Consultation: The loan is integrated into the borrower's overall financial plan.

The client is referred to the Financial Advisor for a cash-flow analysis. *Introduction is best made via email.*

CHAPTER 10

The Financial Advisor
A Plan Tied to Values

The next day, Tom received a call and an e-mail from Michael Conroy, the financial advisor, to schedule an appointment.

Tom was glad to hear from him, but he sighed. "You'll need more paperwork, right?" He thought his right hand would permanently cramp if he had to keep filling out forms.

"Not as much as you might think," Michael chuckled. "In fact, I'd like to have your permission to get your financial information that's on file with Marc. That will give us a big jump ahead in the process. Much of the information I need has already been given to Marc for your pre-approval. It's always easier to do this while you are purchasing a home because many of the documents you are providing to the lender are the same documents I will need."

"You've got it, by all means," Tom said. "Anything that will save me time and effort gets my go-ahead."

"Good, but there is still some additional information I'll need from you. It's a *cash flow analysis.** I'll e-mail it to you. I know Marc probably explained to you what debt lenders consider in these ratios. The cash flow analysis will help us be a little more specific. I would

---

*   For a copy of the cash flow analysis go to *www.whats-your-rate.com*

really appreciate it if you could fill it out and send it back to me before we meet. If you don't know the exact numbers, it's okay. Just do your best."

"Well, okay."

"You'll be glad you did it. I know this may seem like a lot of work, but it will be so beneficial. When lenders make their calculations they don't include certain things that you spend your money on. That's a big missing piece to the puzzle. We're going to figure that out and make you feel much better about this home purchase.

"By the way, I want to congratulate you on selecting Chuck and Marc for your mortgage finance and realtor team. We work together to make sure you have a totally integrated plan and all of your Core 7 advisers are working together so there are no holes in your plan. Marc said you are in need of an accountant and a property and casualty insurance agent also. Once we have them in place, I will coordinate with the accountant to adjust your W-4, and the insurance agent for your homeowner's insurance and umbrella policy."

"Thanks. We know we'll be working with good people."

That night after putting the boys to bed, Tom and Kim sat at the table and worked through Michael's cash flow analysis.

"It's so specific," Kim said, looking through her bank statements and searching for receipts in her wallet. "It feels like tax time again."

"Well, this is really the only way we're going to get ahead—if we know where our money is going every month. I'm sure we'll find some places where we can redirect some spending and start saving for some of our goals."

Michael confirmed Tom's thinking at the appointment a few days later.

"Thank you so much for providing me the cash flow analysis beforehand," he said as he sat down at a conference table with Tom and Kim. He gave them copies of the analysis and began reviewing it with them.

"This shows your spending habits and total cash outlay on a monthly basis. This will give us an idea of what you can spend. As I'm sure Mark mentioned, mortgage lenders only use debt they see on your credit report and your mortgage payment. A cash flow analysis will take into account everything you spend, including entertainment and the basic necessities of life. I was able to do some research and you are doing very well, but I found a few spots where we can make some adjustments."

Tom and Kim looked at each other. What would they have to give up?

"Number one," Michael went on, "we should look at a new cell phone plan and look to pay off the credit card debt you have. Now I know you have a fairly substantial down payment that you are using for your home purchase. My suggestion is we put a little less down and pay off your credit cards with some of that money. The monthly savings you will receive from paying off the cards is much greater than the mortgage payment you will have if you put the extra money down as a larger down payment. And the mortgage interest is tax deductible."

Kim nodded. "That's great. We need to free up some cash flow. As you can probably see, we have a new addition to our family on the way." She ran a hand over the growing roundness of her belly.

"Congratulations," Michael said. "You're right. It's more important than ever to make all of these considerations. I know you've built up a nice down payment, and Marc showed me the total cost analysis he sent with the two pre-approval options: one loan with 3.5 percent down, and the other with all your savings of 10 percent down. The lower down payment option will free up much more cash flow because we can use the extra money to pay off these high-interest credit cards. The net cash flow will be much better this way—the monthly payment on the credit cards is almost double what the savings on the mortgage would be if the money was put toward the down payment. But remember to pay these cards off after the closing, or before you have an accepted offer. Many lenders will want lots of documentation to verify any new inquiries and to make sure you have not taken on any new debt. This could cause delays to the closing.

The Tax Deductibility of Mortgage Interest

$10,000 Credit Card Debt at 5%	$10,000 Mortgage Debt at 5%
= $41.66 per month (not tax deductable)	= $41.66 per month
	After Taxes = $27.08 per month
	Difference = $14.57 per month = $174.92 per year

Disclaimer: Based on a person in the 35% tax bracket

"We need to have a solid foundation before building wealth. When buying a home you need to follow certain principles. So the first priority I want you to consider are cash reserves. After your down payment, plus your closing costs, I'd like to see you have three to six months of your gross income put aside in a safe liquid emergency fund. This will give you a cushion to make it through any setback like a job loss, or if you are injured. Typically if someone is salaried, I recommend three months of reserves, and if someone derives most of their income from bonus income, commission, or is self-employed,

I suggest six months of reserves. However, it also depends on the person. If a salaried employee would sleep better at night with six months of reserves, instead of three, that's okay. This account is for peace of mind."

Salaried W-2 Employee (steady paycheck)	Self-Employed, Commission, or Dependent on Bonus Income
(minimum of 3 months of expenses in reserves)	(minimum of 6 months of expenses in reserves)
example:	*example:*
Total Expenses = $6,000 per month	Total Expenses = $6,000 per month
Amount Needed In Reserve Account:	Amount Needed In Reserve Account:
3 x $6,000 = *$18,000*	6 x $6,000 = *$36,000*

"How do we take that into consideration with our mortgage payment?" Tom wanted to know. "Will the lower down payment affect my rate?"

"Good question. The 10 percent down may be a slightly lower interest rate and a better payment, but sometimes the lowest rate in the wrong product, with the wrong structure and plan can be more expensive than a competitive rate with the proper structure and plan." Michael started writing down some figures for them.

"For example, I have seen many clients put all of their wealth into a house to get the best rate and lowest payment and then have to pull the cash out by refinancing later on in life because they needed money to satisfy other needs. One family that I was working with had prepaid a lot of the principal on their mortgage on a 15-year amortization. Their previous lender recommended the 15-year mortgage because it had a lower interest rate. They were only seven years from paying it off, but at the same time had two kids going to college in the next two years and discovered they couldn't qualify for financial aid. They were forced to take out a home equity line of credit in order to pay for college. Home equity lines are adjustable and can rise to a much higher interest rate. So they were trying to be conservative by doing a 15-year mortgage to pay it off sooner, but ended up taking on more risk."

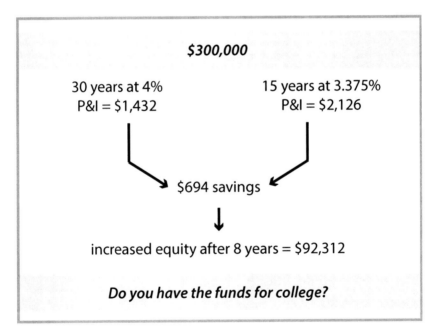

$300,000

30 years at 4%
P&I = $1,432

15 years at 3.375%
P&I = $2,126

$694 savings

increased equity after 8 years = $92,312

Do you have the funds for college?

"Yes, I can see now how something like that can come back to bite you." Tom nodded.

"Good. We need to make sure your overall plan is in place. And as you can see, paying off your mortgage early really doesn't save as much money as most people think. Every $10,000 is approximately $50 a month, and after taxes, that translates to between $30 and $40 a month, depending on what tax bracket you are in. You see, if you are still earning income, mortgage debt can be beneficial."

Tom frowned, a little confused. "Mike, could you show us a break down of that?"

"Let me give you a hypothetical example using a $300,000 loan and a 4.5 percent interest rate. The principal and interest payment is $1,520, and at $10,000 less, the principal and interest is $1,469, for a difference of $51 a month. However, interest is tax deductible, so if you are in the 35 percent tax bracket, the after-tax payment is $1,126 on the $300,000 loan and $1,089 on the $290,000 loan, for a difference of $38 a month.

"The way I look at it is $10,000 is a large sum of money, but $38 dollars a month is very manageable. I'd rather see my clients have $10,000 in reserves than have a $38-a-month lower payment.

The Cost of $10,000

	SUMMARY		
	Program Name	$300,000	$290,000
	Loan Amount	$300,000	$290,000
1st MTG.	Interest Rate	4.5 %	4.5 %
	Term (months)	360	360
	Payment	$1,520	$1,469
	Mtg. Ins.	$0	$0
	Monthy Payment	$1,502	$1,469
	Tax Benefits	$394	$381
	After Tax Payment	$1,126	$1,089
	Net Savings	**$0**	**$38**

Disclaimer: Based on a person in the 35% tax bracket

"By the way, speaking of taxes, I know you're buying right now, but I want you to know that in the future, you can sell your primary residence and receive a tax-free gain of $500,000. The law states that each individual can shelter up to $250,000 per spouse from capital gains tax if you have owned and occupied the property for two of the last five years, another great tax benefit the government uses to promote home ownership.

1997 Tax Payer Relief Act - $250,000/$500,000
Capital Gains Exclusion

If you are filing individually, you can exclude $250,000 of capital gains on the sale of your primary residence.

If you are filing jointly, you can exclude $500,000 of capital gains on the sale of your primary residence.

Disclaimer: Based on a person in the 35% tax bracket.

"But we're not there yet, so let's gets back to real life and look at the numbers from your cash flow analysis," Michael said. "I've calculated this with the lower down payment, all your expenses, and what you will have left over. I think you will be able to maintain your lifestyle while still being able to invest at least 10 percent of your income in other assets. As a rule of thumb I like to see what I call a 70/10/10/10. What I mean by that is 70 percent of your income is for your spending and your bills. Ten percent should be for conservative investments such as retirement, insurance protection, and cash reserves. Ten percent goes to a higher rate of return on investments such as real estate, and 10 percent is for tithing and charitable donations. If you don't mind my saying so, giving to a cause is a great thing to do. It will make you feel good and many times it can come back to you tenfold."

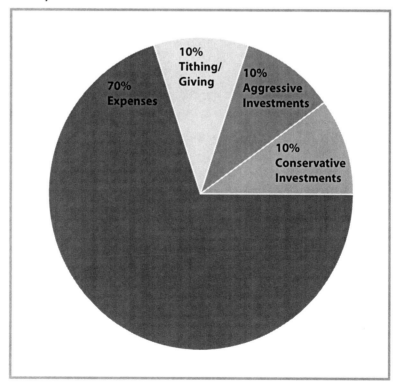

Kim and Tom examined the amount under Michael's 70 percent figure on the total cost analysis and both laughed and breathed a sigh of relief. "That is actually more savings than we expected," Tom said.

"Actually, you could probably qualify for a higher loan amount," Michael pointed out. "But I think the range that you are looking in is your sweet spot. I have seen many people who have purchased too much home, and all of their income goes into the home, and they don't have enough left over for the other investments and protection they need. This can be a dangerous place to be if something unexpected were to happen. People can't invest for the other important things in life because they purchased a home that required the majority of their income. It's usually the first big financial move people make, so they don't even think of the other things."

"Like what?" Tom wanted to know.

"Well, to start," Michael said, "did you know that disability is the number-one reason for foreclosure and bankruptcy?"

Tom looked at Kim and they shook their heads.

"Also, what if your new child is a girl? You would have to think about what her wedding would cost someday. Did you know that according to TheKnot.com the average cost of a wedding—paying for the reception, rings, photography, the wedding gown, music, flowers and invitations—is $28,385? That doesn't include the honeymoon."

"Wow, that's a lot to think about," Tom said. "But you're right. It's important to be ready for events like that. What's next?"

The Cost of a Wedding
from theknot.com

🍴	Reception	$12,838
💍	Rings	$5,847
📷	Photography/Videography	$3,925
👛	Miscellaneous	$696
👔	Wedding Gown	$1,134
💿	Music	$1,343
🌷	Flowers & Decor	$2,093
✉	Invitations	$509
🧾	*Total*	***$28,385***

(excluding the honeymoon!)

"Before we move on, I'd like to reaffirm that we are in agreement that the price range you're looking at is right for you. Do you both agree?"

Tom and Kim nodded. "Yes, sounds good to us," said Kim.

"Great. Now I'd like to talk about your values and goals," Michael replied. "Sometimes this can be a difficult conversation, but nothing could be more important. What you do, what you plan for, must be tied to your core values for you to be truly happy. There are many people who have a lot of money, but do not feel complete.

All the money in the world can't make them happy because it's not connected to what they care about. In many cases, people act out and do things that end up in divorce, and sometimes even worse.

"The best example I can give of this is what happened to Howard Hughes. He had everything that money could buy, but he ended up abusing drugs and living in isolation, in a hotel room, with five-inch fingernails and hair down to his knees. You don't want to end up with a house full of material things, expensive cars in your garage, and no meaning in your life. If your values are clear, your decisions are easy."

Tom and Kim nodded, but they really didn't know what to expect in the exercise.

"Okay, who wants to go first?" Michael asked.

Tom shrugged. "I guess I will."

"All right, Tom." Michael flipped to a fresh sheet of paper on his legal pad. "Money can mean a lot of things to different people. Help me understand what's important about money to you."

Tom thought for a moment. "Well, we need money so we'll be able to pay for things."

"Okay." Michael wrote down what Tom had said. "If you are able to pay for things, what would that accomplish for you?"

Tom felt a little perturbed. Wasn't that obvious? "If we could pay for things, then we wouldn't have to worry."

Michael smiled reassuringly. "I told you this might be difficult, but trust me. I went through this process with my financial coach and mentor, and it absolutely changed my life. Stick with me here."

"You have a coach and advisor too?" Kim asked, surprised.

"Yes, I do," Michael replied. "Everyone can use help, even professionals. No one can possibly stay in tune with every aspect of his or her financial well being by themselves. Life gets in the way. Now, the importance of money usually comes down to more than things or events. It's much more emotional, and really has to do with your core values. The reason this may be hard is because most people never think about these things. So if it's okay, I'd like to continue on with the questions."

"Oh, it's fine," Tom said. "This all makes sense to me. My frustration is not with you, Michael. It's just that I'm beginning to realize how much I'm not sure of. I've just been going through life blindly with no roadmap."

"Well, we're working on that map right now. Don't beat yourself up too much, Tom. A Harvard study found that only 3 percent of people have written goals. So, if you had plenty of money to buy things, what would that give you?"

"I feel that I would not have to worry about anything. I would feel secure, and could relax and enjoy my family and create memories."

"So security, family, and creating memories are important to you?" Michael asked.

"Yes, those are very important to me. If anything were to happen to me, I need my family to be cared for. I wouldn't want them to suffer in any way. And I'd like them to feel that I did right by them as a provider."

"Now that's a value," Michael said. He wrote "Security/Family/ Memories" under the heading, Values, on his paper. "Values are much more than things. Typically I like to get three to five values down before we start discussing goals, so let's keep going. If you had security and then were able to focus on creating memories with your family, what does that give you?"

Tom took another moment to think. "A happy family. Now that would make me fulfilled. I'd want to know that I've made a difference in my family's life even after I'm gone."

"So family and personal fulfillment that you've made a difference is important to you?"

"Yes."

Mike continued to write. "Those are true values: security, family, and personal fulfillment that you've made a difference. That's great."

Michael continued questioning Tom until they had completed the list of Tom's values. By the time they were done, Michael had written down: security, making a difference/creating a legacy, family, and personal fulfillment. Michael then took Kim through the values exercise. Tom and Kim were happy to discover they shared most of the same values. The only difference was that Kim wanted the excitement of travel and felt it was important to get away to relax. So excitement and fun made her list of values. She added that if they ever bought a second home, she wanted it to be near the water. "That would be a great place for building memories with the family," she said.

"Wait! I want that too," Tom chimed in. "Add excitement and fun to my list too." He was already envisioning going fishing with his children, teaching them to swim, and building sand castles. He also saw himself sitting back with Kim and having a drink on the beach. He could almost smell the salt in the sea air.

"You got it," Michael said. "The reason I'm writing this down is that one of the most important things is that we track this, and revisit your values on an ongoing basis. Consistently reviewing these values and staying focused on the goals we attach to them will make it much more likely we will achieve them. I always keep a file on everything I ever speak with my clients about. I want to make sure that all my clients' decisions are tied in with their values. Many times when some of my clients experience success, they lose track of what's important. They start to want material things that have no real value.

Now don't get me wrong. It is nice to have luxuries, but not just because you have the money to do it. We do a review of their values at every meeting and that usually gives them focus and keeps them on the right track. It's always great when we review the values exercise from the years past. It's amazing how it really brings things to light and gets people to focus on what's really important. Does that make sense?"

"Absolutely," Tom and Kim said in unison.

"This will also help as you review your investment activity," Michael pointed out. "Many financial advisers get caught up in only focusing on returns, and then their clients end up leaving them when they experience losses. Losses happen in every market. It is impossible to make accurate predictions because no one can control the market. But if we stay focused on our goals, on what we are trying to achieve, and why we are invested the way we are, it will all fall into place. What I really want to stress is that we are going to experience the ups and downs of the market. In our meeting, after you close on your home, I'm going to show you how we will strategically mitigate those ups and downs. You are going to get frustrated if you experience losses and maybe even a little greedy if you get big returns, but we are always going to stay in line with your values, okay?"

"Yes," Tom nodded. "It makes so much sense. I can see how things can get out of focus."

Kim agreed. "It always amazes me how all of these celebrities who have all this money can get into trouble or abuse drugs and be unhappy. I bet it's because they are not clear on their values."

"I'd say nine times out of ten you're probably right," Michael said. "All the money in the world will not make people happy if they don't know what their purpose in life is and why they are doing what they do. Everyone needs something to live for. This is why I also want you to think of what I call a 'dream goal'—something to really shoot for, but would be shocked if you ever achieved—a trip around the world with your entire family, starting a charitable foundation, or climbing Mt. Everest. Do you understand what I'm getting at?"

Tom nodded, already thinking. He wasn't sure exactly what a huge dream goal for him would be, but he was pretty sure it would be connected to his desire to make a difference. He was going to have to work on that one.

Michael stood up and reached over to shake their hands. "Okay, that's it for now. I'll analyze everything we did today and we'll meet again after the home closing to put together a full plan that is based on your core values. For now, just concentrate on finding the right home for you. The only thing I'll add is to make sure you stay in the price range we discussed, so you will have enough cash flow left over to meet some of your other goals. If anything changes, make sure you call me so we can re-evaluate."

As they left Michael's office, Tom grabbed Kim's hand and squeezed it. She looked up at him.

"What are you feeling right now?" she wanted to know.

"Clear—just really, finally, absolutely clear." An overwhelming feeling of emotion came over him. "I really feel I have a purpose and some direction now. I know what I'm fighting for, what I'm working so hard for. I am finally clear."

Tom decided he didn't want to wait until he got home. He pulled out his phone and called John to share with him what he and Kim had learned.

"It makes a big difference, doesn't it?" John asked.

"Oh yes, all the difference in the world," said Tom. "I can't believe we were trying to do this before without this kind of support. There are a few extra steps, but it's worth it."

"Have you found a house yet?"

"No, we're looking again with Chuck this weekend. But even looking for houses is different. It's fun because we know what we're looking for and what we can afford. I think it's going to be a lot easier to find our home now."

"Well, I'll be sorry to lose you as a neighbor, but I know this is going to be great for you. Come by and have coffee when you have pictures of your new place. I want to hear all about it."

As Tom hung up, he thought about how much he still wanted to be in touch with John, even after they moved. He couldn't imagine being without his new and valued friend.

Review

CHAPTER 6

Referral is given to Realtor. The best introductions are made via email with both the Realtor and client copied.

CHAPTER 7

Realtor makes appointment at the office.
Buyer meeting at the Realtor's office.
Realtor refers the Mortgage Originator.

CHAPTER 8

Mortgage Originator sets an appointment with the client for a loan consultation. Pre-consultation worksheets are filled out prior to the consultation and analyzed by the Mortgage Originator.

CHAPTER 9

The Loan Consultation: The loan is integrated into the borrower's overall financial plan.
The client is referred to the Financial Advisor for a cash-flow analysis.
Introduction is best made via email.

CHAPTER 10

Cash-flow analysis is reviewed by the Financial Advisor and client.

Values Ascertation: "Finding out what's really important."

Ready to Buy

When Tom and Kim headed out for the next round of house hunting, they felt so confident they decided to take Tommy Jr. and Ben with them. They were careful to explain that they hoped to find a better house for them than the one they had seen before.

"We really need your help, guys," Tom told them. "We might have to look at a few places today. You don't have to like them all. In fact, it'll be just as important for you to tell us what you don't like. Do you understand?"

They nodded excitedly. "Let's go!"

"Okay, let's get in the car," Kim said. "We have to meet Chuck at the first house. He's going to help us look."

Once they had the kids loaded in the car, they hit the road. The day went just as their previous one had. At the first property, they met Chuck, and he handed them a packet with listing sheets of all the properties they were going to see that day. They visited a variety of properties in several neighborhoods. The boys were surprisingly well behaved. Tom thought, "I guess they really appreciate being part of the process."

"The next house I am really excited for you to see," Chuck said, pointing out the next listing sheet in their packet. They followed him there.

"Oh, this is nice," Kim said, examining the photo. The house had yellow siding with little window boxes below the front windows.

"Yes, but there's one particular reason I want you to see this one," Chuck said.

Tom turned onto the street and drove down to a huge circle at the end of the road. The house they were going to see was right there.

"See?" said Chuck. "There's more than one cul-de-sac in the area. I noted from our meeting how much you liked the idea of a cul-de-sac so that the kids could play. It's actually a lot like the house you previously had under agreement."

"Cool," Tom said as the car pulled into the driveway. He already had a good feeling about the place.

"Now, before we go in," Chuck said as he parked the car, "here are some quick guidelines on what questions to ask and what not to ask when you are at an open house or a showing of a home. We don't want to point out any defects to the listing agent or ask any questions about the ages of systems. We can discuss those points privately."

"Why not?" Kim wanted to know.

"Well, for example, if we notice that the roof is older, we do not want to ask, 'How old is the roof?' If the agent tells us it is twenty-five years old, we could potentially lose our rights at inspection. When the inspector tells us that the roof is at end of life, we will not be able to ask the seller for a credit. Technically, they had already told us it was twenty-five years old, which is the life expectancy of a roof. The other side will tell us that we knew the roof was old and should have made our offer accordingly. If we don't ask for the specific age of systems, the inspection report will be 'new' information for us, and we can negotiate accordingly after inspection. The only questions we want to ask are the ones that will help us decide whether or not to make an offer. For example, if gas cooking is important, we should ask if there is gas in the house or on the street, but not how old the stove is. Make sense?"

"A lot of sense," Kim said and Tom nodded. "Thank you Chuck. Marc mentioned that negotiating was one of your strengths."

"Good. Let's go in."

Walking through the front door, Tom and Kim marveled at how homey the house already felt. It was a little smaller than the house they'd seen all those weeks ago, but it had similar features: warm paint tones, an open floor plan, a bright kitchen. There was even a fireplace in the family room.

Tom followed the boys upstairs to look at the bedrooms. Ben ran up and down the hall as he had done in the other homes, but Tommy Jr. moved slowly from room to room and looked out of each window. He came back to Tom and took his hand. "Daddy," he whispered. "I really like this place."

Tom smiled and nodded. "I do too."

They continued going through the rest of the house. It had a finished basement and a small deck that looked out onto a swing set in the backyard. When they were done with the showing, they went back to Chuck's office to discuss all of the properties, especially this one. Before Tom and Kim got into their car to go to Chuck's office, Chuck pointed out the positives and negatives of the house and asked, "Can you see yourself living here? Take the time to think about that in the car on the way over to my office."

Once they arrived at Chuck's office, Tom and Kim felt they had an answer. "Chuck, we really think this is it," Tom said, as they piled around the conference table in Chuck's office.

"I had a feeling you'd like it. So, just in case, I have already done what is called a CMA or price analysis." Chuck opened his bag and took out some paperwork. He reviewed the pricing strategy moving forward. "Do you want to write an offer?"

"We can go a little lower than the asking price, right?" Kim asked.

"Yes. Remember, it's price and terms. Everything is negotiable. If we offer the seller a lower price, we should give them better terms. The property has been on the market over a hundred days, so I expect that we can get a good price. The listing price is a starting point. Where do you think you want to start?" Chuck replied.

Tom suggested a number a little lower than what they had discussed with Michael and Marc.

"Okay," said Chuck. "And we are going to ask for something called a seller concession, so that you'll need less cash to purchase this home."

"Really?" Tom was impressed. "How does that work, Chuck? Marc mentioned you would discuss this."

"Essentially, this allows you to finance your closing costs and bring less money to the table. It is often misunderstood. What we do is increase the purchase price with the seller paying the closing costs and other related funds needed. It's a paper transaction to the seller. So, let's say that we negotiate a $300,000 purchase price. We would increase the price to $305,000 with the seller credit of $5,000. It will cost you approximately $25 a month to do this. Still there's a net price of $300,000 to the seller. However, these funds must 'wash' against your closing costs and your pre-paids. There is also typically a limit of 3 percent of the purchase price. Many agents and sellers don't fully understand how this works, so I write into the offer, 'buyer has the right to finance closing costs,' and then after we have negotiated the price, you have the option of doing this. We just need to determine that prior to signing the purchase and sale agreement

(P&S), and make sure that the appraisal supports the new purchase price.

"Marc and I have discussed this strategy, and he is aware we might want to do this. So let's back up for a moment and discuss what these costs are. When you purchase a home, there is a certain amount of money that is needed up front, other than your down payment. There are closing costs, maybe points if you choose to buy your interest rate down, your escrow account, and some pre-paid interest, which is per day so it depends on what day you close on your home.

"Let's say for example you were buying a $300,000 home and putting 5 percent down, which is $15,000. You will also have an escrow account, which typically contains three to six months of property taxes, two to three months of property insurance, two months of mortgage insurance if your loan requires it, plus your per diem interest, which is from your closing till the end of the month. This is why most people try to close on the last day of the month. Frankly, you aren't saving any money by doing this, so my team and I usually recommend closing in the middle of the month, to avoid a scheduling log jam. At our buyers meeting we discussed that you are tenants-at-will, so you need to give your landlord thirty days notice. We want to build in some time for you to move comfortably, so let's aim to close on the twentieth. Does that make sense?

"There are also optional, but highly recommended, attorneys fees, which your real estate attorney, whom I will refer to you, will explain in detail. They are your purchase and sale fee, and owner's title insurance. So let's say altogether these extras are $5,000. Instead of paying out-of-pocket, we offer the seller a $305,000 purchase price with a $5,000 seller concession for pre-paids and closing costs. It's key that it reads like this because seller concessions can only go toward points, prepaids, and closing costs. It is also important that we negotiate this up front so there are no surprises for anyone. If we try to do this after the purchase and sale, a lender may not allow us to increase the purchase price after it has already been agreed upon. We may also have an appraisal problem if we wait. It's very easy to finance less and decrease purchase price after an offer is accepted, but it is very difficult to increase it.

SUMMARY		
Program Name	**Paying the Cost**	**Seller Concession**
Loan Amount	$285,000	$289,750
Interest Rate	4.5 %	4.5 %
Term (months)	360	360
Payment	$1,444	$1,468
Mtg. Ins.	$0	$0
Monthy Payment	$1,444	$1,488
Tax Benefits	$374	$380
After Tax Payment	$1,070	$1,088
Net Savings	$18	$0

1st MTG.

TOTAL COST ANALYSIS		
Program Name	**Paying the Cost**	**Seller Concession**
Total Payment	$519,859	$528,523
Principal Paid	$285,000	$289,750
Int & MI Paid	$234,859	$238,773
Balance Left	$0	$0
Closing & Points	$5,000	$0
Total Cost	$239,859	$238,773
Tax Benefits	$82,201	$83,571
After Tax Cost	$157,658	$155,203
Net Savings	$0	$2,456

360 MONTHS ANALYSIS

"There are also no points and no closing cost loans when you take a slightly higher interest rate. The lender pays these costs for you. This may make sense for you, but it is something you should go over with Marc. If you do decide to go this route, it would be possible to knock the cost of the repairs off the purchase price after the fact and bring it back to $300,000. The only thing to keep in mind is the property has to appraise at the 'new' purchase price with the seller concession. A good listing agent will agree to this, but only if it appraises for that value. If that doesn't happen, you would need to pay the closing costs out of pocket, or do a true no-points, no-closing-cost loan.

The important piece is that it will make it less necessary to have a fixed amount of money up front. You could keep the savings in your reserves for furniture, you could invest it, or use it however you see fit. A seller concession has no impact on the seller's profit, and is very common. The interest you pay is tax deductible, so it makes sense."

"Well, it sounds like a great strategy," Tom said, looking at Kim. She nodded. "Okay, let's do that."

Chuck filled out the forms and Tom and Kim signed them. Tom wrote out a check for the deposit. "Funny," he thought, "I'm not worried about losing that one."

"Have we bought the house now?" Tommy Jr. and Ben wanted to know.

"No, this is just the beginning," Tom explained. "If all goes well, it will be our home."

"Okay, so let's review what happens next. First, you will wake up tomorrow morning in a little bit of a panic. It's called buyer's remorse, and it is totally normal. The majority of my first time homebuyers experience this. Please don't worry. If we find a real problem, we'll cancel the transaction and get all of your money back.

Regarding the offer, there are four possible responses. First, they can accept it outright. This is unlikely because our offer price is below the asking price. Two, they can reject it and not respond. That is possible, but I'll push to get a counteroffer. Three, they can give us a token counter, just to show they are willing to negotiate, something around $1,000–$2,000. Last, is a real counter, somewhere in the $5,000–$10,000 range. That's what we are hoping for. Please keep in mind, that as soon as they counter, it's technically a rejection of our offer, and our offer is null and void at that point. You will have no obligation to move forward."

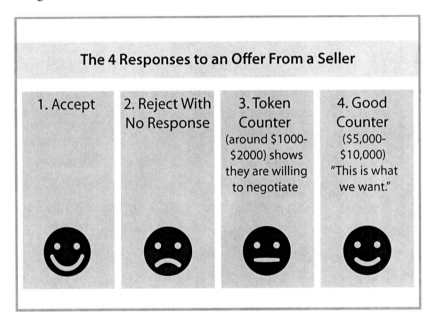

The 4 Responses to an Offer From a Seller

| 1. Accept | 2. Reject With No Response | 3. Token Counter (around $1000–$2000) shows they are willing to negotiate | 4. Good Counter ($5,000–$10,000) "This is what we want." |

Tom was surprised when the phone rang that evening and he found Chuck on the other line. "Okay, I have good news about your offer."

"Already?"

"Yes, the sellers have a counter—and it's a real counter, not just a token response."

"Really?" Tom wasn't a big fan of going back and forth and was slightly put off.

"They want $5,000 more. What do you think about that?"

Tom called Kim to the phone and expressed his concern. "They're going to hassle us for $5,000?"

"It's okay, Tom," Chuck said. "This is entirely reasonable. We discussed this. It is very unlikely that a seller will accept the first offer unless it's right at the asking price. And, if they had accepted our first offer, you would always wonder if you could have gotten it for less. Our strategy was designed to come in on the low side and see where we were. Five thousand is better than I expected. My sense from the other agent is that the seller wanted to counter higher, but after I told her I wasn't sure how much higher you would go, we got to a number that can make sense."

"It's okay, Tom," Kim said. "Remember, this is why we hired Chuck in the first place. He's looking out for us here, so let him do what he does best, and get us the best deal possible. And remember what we learned from Marc: every $10,000 of mortgage is only about $40 a month after taxes. After going through the cash flow analysis with Michael, we know that we are buying in our comfort zone. We shouldn't let our egos get in the way now."

"You're right," Tom agreed. "I am just letting my ego get in the way. Go ahead, Chuck, and accept the counteroffer, and let's see what they say."

Chuck phoned again the next day, just as the family was finishing breakfast.

"We have an accepted offer," he reported.

"They accepted it," Tom called out.

"What? What?" Tommy Jr. and Ben shouted.

"It means we're gonna get to buy the house."

"Yay! Yippee! We're gonna have our own yard."

Tom and Kim hugged, but then Tom heard Chuck still on the line.

"Tom? Tom?"

"Sorry, Chuck, we got a little carried away here," Tom said, putting the phone back to his ear.

"That's okay. Congratulations! Now there are several things we need to do next and I wanted to go over them with you."

Tom grabbed a sheet of paper to write on. "Fire away."

"I need you to get in touch with Marc, and Josh Rodman, the attorney I referred, right away. We have some very important dates to keep an eye on, and we need to move at a good pace to make sure you make your commitment date. The first two weeks are always the busiest. I am going to send an e-mail with all of this information and I'll cc everyone on your team, so we'll all be in the loop.

"I am happy to set up an inspection with a home inspector. What times and dates work for you both? Would it be too much trouble to arrange childcare, so you both can be focused? We need to do the inspection within seven days."

Tom felt a little scared. This must be the natural buyer's remorse that Chuck had told him about, but for the most part he was hugely excited.

When Tom arrived home later that day, Kim showed him two personal notes that she had received in the mail from Marc and Chuck thanking them for their business. What a nice touch. He couldn't help thinking that this was what the process was really supposed to feel like.

Review

CHAPTER 6

Referral is given to Realtor. The best introductions are made via email with both the Realtor and client copied.

CHAPTER 7

Realtor makes appointment at the office.
Buyer meeting at the Realtor's office.
Realtor refers the Mortgage Originator.

CHAPTER 8

Mortgage Originator sets an appointment with the client for a loan consultation. Pre-consultation worksheets are filled out prior to the consultation and analyzed by the Mortgage Originator.

CHAPTER 9

The Loan Consultation: The loan is integrated into the borrower's overall financial plan.
The client is referred to the Financial Advisor for a cash-flow analysis.
Introduction is best made via email.

CHAPTER 10

Cash-flow analysis is reviewed by the Financial Advisor and client.
Values Ascertation: "Finding out what's really important."

CHAPTER 11

If loan is approved by underwriting a pre-approval letter is issued.

Search for property begins.

Make an offer.

Realtor refers Real Estate Attorney for Purchase & Sale review.

Schedule home inspection.

The Real Estate Attorney

The phone in Tom's office rang the following morning just after his coffee break. Tom was pleased to find a friendly voice on the other end when he picked it up.

"Hello Tom. I'm Josh Rodman, the real estate attorney Chuck told you about. Thank you so much for the opportunity to represent you. Have you ever worked with an attorney before?"

"Honestly, no I haven't," Tom said as he leaned back in his office chair. "It seems that whenever I see lawyers on television, people are paying them huge retainers and big hourly fees."

"Yeah, some lawyers do work that way." Josh laughed. "But simple real estate transactions are often just a flat fee. By the way, I have something for you. It's a check refunding your $1,000 deposit from your original deal."

Tom nearly fell out of his seat. "How did you get it back?" he said breathlessly.

"Deposit funds are usually kept in escrow and the sellers hadn't taken possession of it yet. I had a talk with the realtor and she knew she hadn't proceeded fairly and you had no representation at the time. They really had no choice but to give it back. You had not even signed a purchase and sale. If they chose to fight us on it, I could have held them up from finding another buyer, as you might not have 'released' them. The deposit release, which I'll send you to sign, releases each party from the other."

"Oh my goodness!" Tom couldn't wait to tell Kim. "I can't believe it. We thought that money was gone forever. How can I thank you?"

"No need to thank me. It's what I do."

"Actually," Tom said, shifting in his chair, "I don't really understand what a real estate attorney does. Can you tell me?"

"Of course, I'd be happy to. Real estate transactions can be tricky business, as you learned yourself. They are sometimes difficult if you don't have legal assistance. I basically take you through the process of the transfer of ownership for the property. I also make sure that you are protected in all parts of the process, especially the contingency dates."

"Okay, but how do you do that?" Tom asked.

"I will review all of the documents in the transaction including the sales contract and all the mortgage documents. The devil is in the details. I also check the title, which is the chain of ownership for the property, to make sure you will own it without liens or any other claims on the home. Title insurance insures the title or ownership rights to a piece of property, guaranteeing that the property being purchased is free from undisclosed liens and any confusion regarding ownership will be resolved in favor of the party buying the real estate. Lender's title insurance is required by all lenders and protects the lender. Owner's title insurance protects you, the owner, ensuring that you have a good, marketable title to the property, free and clear of any liens or encumbrances. In many cases I'm asked if it's necessary for owners to purchase title insurance. I highly recommend it for the following reasons: First, the premium for purchase of the title insurance policy is a one-time charge. However, the coverage stays in effect for as long as you own the home. Second, you, as the buyer, have the opportunity at the time of closing to obtain an owner's policy at a cost substantially less than you would pay if the policy were not written simultaneously with the lender's policy at the time of closing. Third and most important, owner's title insurance protects you against a variety of problems that could surface in the future."

"Could you give me a couple of examples of how we could lose our home if we don't have owner's title insurance?" Tom asked.

"Of course," Josh said. "There could have been forged documents in the title or undischarged liens or mortgages attached to the property, which is very common today, especially with several mortgage companies going out of business. Mistakes or inaccuracies in the recording of the legal documents of title at the appropriate place are common these days. All of the legal papers in the transaction have to be verified and filed by an attorney, so I would do that as well.

"But what may be the biggest part of protecting you is I make sure the right contingency language goes into all of your contracts, which I will work on with Marc and Chuck. For example, you'll want a clause in your sales contract that itemizes the inspection items, to make sure they are done in a good workmanlike manner. We will explain all these loan documents. They are standard documents that all buyers sign."

Tom nodded. "Chuck mentioned that you would keep track of our deadlines too, like the date when we have to have a mortgage commitment. Is that right?"

"Correct, if you choose to have me represent you," said Josh. "In fact, Chuck's team and I will make sure that all the paperwork flows smoothly so I'll know what's on track and can give you a heads up if it looks as if things aren't happening on schedule. If we need an extension, for any reason, I'll work with the seller's attorney. Extensions are fairly common, and the goal is to make sure your deposit is protected."

"Sounds good," Tom said.

"That was painless," Tom thought later that day as he was on his way home. He couldn't wait to tell Kim and suggest they take the kids out for dinner that evening. He realized he hadn't felt that good since Kim had told him she was pregnant. That day seemed a lifetime ago now.

Then he caught himself. "What would Michael say about going out to dinner?" Tom wondered. "Forget it! We're celebrating. I'll deal with the financial planning when the time comes."

But he also knew full well that his meeting with Michael was taking place very soon.

Review

CHAPTER 6

Referral is given to Realtor. The best introductions are made via email with both the Realtor and client copied.

CHAPTER 7

Realtor makes appointment at the office.
Buyer meeting at the Realtor's office.
Realtor refers the Mortgage Originator.

CHAPTER 8

Mortgage Originator sets an appointment with the client for a loan consultation. Pre-consultation worksheets are filled out prior to the consultation and analyzed by the Mortgage Originator.

CHAPTER 9

The Loan Consultation: The loan is integrated into the borrower's overall financial plan.
The client is referred to the Financial Advisor for a cash-flow analysis.
Introduction is best made via email.

CHAPTER 10

Cash-flow analysis is reviewed by the Financial Advisor and client.
Values Ascertation: "Finding out what's really important."

CHAPTER 11

If loan is approved by underwriting a pre-approval letter is issued.
Search for property begins.
Make an offer.
Realtor refers Real Estate Attorney for Purchase & Sale review.
Schedule home inspection.

CHAPTER 12

Attorney reviews offer.

Attorney reviews their role in the process and the importance of the contigency dates and owner's title.

The Re-consultation
Firming Up the Details

Tom and Kim were very excited about Marc's call. They were eager to discuss the actual numbers they would be working with, now that they knew which home they were buying. They were also pleased that this discussion would take place by phone.

"First of all, let me say congratulations," Marc began. "It's great when you've finally found the place you want. Now let me give you a quick agenda of how this call will go. First, we will firm up our mortgage strategy based on this particular property. Second, we will discuss rate movement, the mortgage-backed securities market, and rate locking. And last, I will e-mail a total cost analysis showing a side-by-side comparison, addressing the options we've discussed.

"At pre-approval you were most comfortable with a 30-year fixed mortgage loan because you planned on staying in this home for more than thirty years, were looking for a home that needed no extra work, and wanted to know what your exact monthly payment would be so you could have a set monthly budget. Is this still the case?"

"Yes," Tom and Kim said in unison. "We have found the exact house we were looking for."

Marc said, "Great! Congratulations!"

Marc went on, "Now do you remember our discussion at pre-approval on how rates are based on the mortgage bond market and can change multiple times per day based on market activity?"

Tom shook his head sheepishly. "Not really. I was just thinking about pre-approval at the time. However, I did read the article you sent this morning on how and why rates move. Can we go over that?"

"No problem," Marc said. "It's really simple: good economic news is bad for interest rates and bad economic news is good for interest rates. Sounds a little backward, doesn't it? For example, last week, the unemployment report came in better than expected. It was great for the stock market but not for the bond market, so rates went up. But then, two days ago, retail sales came in much lower than expected, which is bad news for the economy. So the stock market went down and the bond market went up. As a result, interest rates went down. So all you have to remember is good economic news is bad for interest rates, bad economic news is good for interest rates. Because of this volatility, rates can change at any time. It's smart to lock in a good rate and payment that you are comfortable with when it's available. So after you review the total cost analysis that I'll e-mail you, we'll discuss whether you want to lock or float your rate.

"It's important to know that if you lock, you need to consider the length of your lock period. Knowing your exact closing date becomes very important. For example, if your closing is thirty days away, you need to lock for thirty days. If your closing is thirty-seven days away, a 30-day lock will not be enough time; you will need to lock for forty-five days.

"Because the mortgage bond market is constantly moving, the longer the investors have to honor a certain rate for you, the more risk they assume. A 45-day lock can typically have a slightly higher interest rate than a 30-day rate lock, and a 60-day rate lock can have a slightly higher rate than a 45-day rate lock. Does this make sense?

A Rate Sheet May Look Like This
The rate spread is not guaranteed

15 Day Lock	30 Day Lock	45 Day Lock	60 Day Lock
4.375	4.5	4.625	4.75

"Some of my clients like to lock right away because they don't want to worry about it, and some of my clients like to gamble and watch the market as long as they can up until the closing. Typically, lenders require you to lock within five to ten business days before your closing. I do my best to educate buyers on what's going on in the market, and when the best time is to lock. However, it is impossible for someone to predict the market 100 percent of the time. Either way, the key is to figure out a comfortable monthly payment that you are satisfied with. I am a fan of locking in if you are happy with the rate and payment. If interest rates were to drop significantly, there is always the possibility of refinancing after closing. If you don't lock and rates go up, there is the possibility that they may never come back down."

Tom asked, "What if we lock in and rates go down before we close? Can we get the new rate?"

"That's a great question, and I'm glad you asked," Marc replied. "Once you lock your rate, you are locked. Your rate cannot go higher or lower. Because of the market volatility we discussed, interest rates are going to change many times after you lock in. But the rate and corresponding payment that you have secured cannot change. That's the good news.

"There is something called a float down option, where you could relock at a lower price if rates dropped before closing. There is always a cost to this, whether it is built into the rate or fully disclosed. Some lenders say they have a no-cost float down when what they are actually doing is resubmitting the loan to a different lender. This is very dangerous because you will be starting the entire process all over again. I have seen many commitment dates missed because of this practice.

"So what I'm going to do now is prepare the total cost analysis of the loan structure we discussed, including the seller concession. It will break down your exact rate and payment, including tax benefits, over the life of the loan. I am going to e-mail it to you shortly and am also going to copy Michael, your financial advisor, so we can make sure the structure fits into your overall financial plan."

Tom and Kim reviewed Marc's analysis with Michael that night and agreed they were satisfied with locking in the current rate. They were very comfortable with the payment and didn't want to be greedy. Tom also remembered that .125 percent was equal to a caramel macchiato. "And besides," he said to Marc the next day when he called to lock, "we can refinance at any time, right?"

"Absolutely. I'll lock you in right away and send you an e-mail confirmation that we have secured that rate."

"That would be great. Thank you, Marc."

Review

CHAPTER 6

Referral is given to realtor. The best introductions are made via email with both the Realtor and client copied.

CHAPTER 7

Realtor makes appointment at the office.
Buyer meeting at the Realtor's office.
Realtor refers the Mortgage Originator.

CHAPTER 8

Mortgage Originator sets an appointment with the client for a loan consultation. Pre-consultation worksheets are filled out prior to the consultation and analyzed by the Mortgage Originator.

CHAPTER 9

The Loan Consultation: The loan is integrated into the borrower's overall financial plan.
The client is referred to the Financial Advisor for a cash-flow analysis.
Introduction is best made via email.

CHAPTER 10

Cash-flow analysis is reviewed by the Financial Advisor and client.
Values Ascertation: "Finding out what's really important."

CHAPTER 11

If loan is approved by underwriting a pre-approval letter is issued.
Search for property begins.
Make an offer.
Realtor refers Real Estate Attorney for Purchase & Sale review.
Schedule home inspection.

CHAPTER 12

Attorney reviews offer.
Attorney reviews their role in the process and the importance of the contigency dates and owner's title.

CHAPTER 13

Lender puts loan into process (appraisal and title are ordered and necessary documents are gathered) and re-consultation is scheduled to firm up the details of the loan structure.

Re-consultation: Details are firmed up regarding new property and desired loan structre. Communication is made with client's existing network to make sure the plan is aligned (referral is made to Property & Casualty Agent).

CHAPTER 14

The Property and Casualty Insurance Agent

Vital Protection from Lawsuits

A few days after Tom and Kim's meeting with Marc, Tom received an e-mail from Marc's office with an introduction to Phyllis Maiocca, the insurance agent Marc had referred them to. Tom called Phyllis and put her on speaker, so Kim could listen in as well. They were both eager to understand the insurance piece. Tom didn't know anything about insurance aside from the coverage he had for his car and his family's health insurance.

"Can I ask a stupid question?" Tom said into the phone after exchanging pleasantries. "I think I get the property part. We're buying a house, so that's property. But what exactly is casualty insurance?"

"That's not a stupid question," Phyllis said. "Most people don't understand it, but the stupid thing is they don't ask the question until it's too late. Casualty insurance insures against accidents that aren't necessarily tied to any specific property. It's actually a broad spectrum of insurance that could include auto, workers compensation, and some liability insurances.

"Your car insurance is really one of the most common kinds of casualty insurance. It provides liability coverage in the event that a driver is found 'at fault' in an accident. The insurance can cover medical expenses of individuals involved in the accident, as well as restitution or repair of any damaged property."

"Okay, that's clearer than I expected it to be. I even already have casualty insurance." Tom laughed.

"Yes, it's not that complicated," Phyllis said. "I think people make it harder than it really is. The real question is how much insurance do you need?"

"How do we figure that out?" Kim asked.

"Well, the information I've received from Marc, your loan officer, and Michael, your financial planner, will help us do that. We have to look at your unique financial situation and consider both the liability and property damage portions of your policy. You don't want to be undercovered, but at the same time you don't want to have too much and wind up paying for way more coverage than you need.

"It's usually recommended that you purchase as much home-owner's insurance as you can afford. Your lender will require that you carry an amount equal to 100 percent of the replacement costs of the property being insured. But if you don't have a lot of assets to protect—in the event someone is severely injured or killed on your property, or if you damage another's property—you may be able to get away with the lowest liability coverage offered."

"But our situation can change, right?" said Tom.

"Right. Ideally your financial situation will improve over the years and your coverage should change along with it. When you become what we call a 'high net worth individual,' you have a lot to lose and you need to protect it. A $500,000 liability limit would likely be your minimum option then. It is also highly recommended that you purchase a personal umbrella policy in addition to your existing home and auto insurance policies, to make sure you are as protected as possible."

"Yes, Marc and Michael told us to discuss umbrella policies with you," Tom remembered.

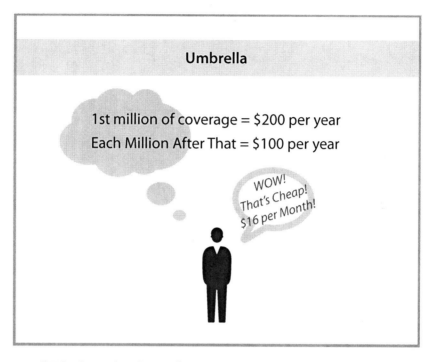

"Which is why they refer me exclusively," Phyllis said. "I always coordinate with your team to make sure the rest of your assets are protected. One bad lawsuit could wipe you out if you don't have the proper coverage in place. If you are sued, you may be forced to pay a legal judgment from your current assets and future earnings. Your umbrella policy can also pay for your legal defense costs, which can add up even if you win the case. I recommend a $1 million umbrella policy if you earn over $100,000 a year or have over $1 million in assets, and a $3–$5 million policy if you own rental property. The cost is typically $200 a year for the first million and $100 a year for each million after that. Now let's look at your situation and what might be the best for you. I will review these coverage amounts with Michael, your financial advisor, to make sure all of your assets are protected. We'll be renewing your policy every year, so we will always adjust accordingly."

By the end of the session, Phyllis had helped them plan their coverage and Tom was again feeling very satisfied. He was confident this feeling would be the norm from then on.

Review

CHAPTER 6

Referral is given to realtor. The best introductions are made via email with both the Realtor and client copied.

CHAPTER 7

Realtor makes appointment at the office.
Buyer meeting at the Realtor's office.
Realtor refers the Mortgage Originator.

CHAPTER 8

Mortgage Originator sets an appointment with the client for a loan consultation. Pre-consultation worksheets are filled out prior to the consultation and analyzed by the Mortgage Originator.

CHAPTER 9

The Loan Consultation: The loan is integrated into the borrower's overall financial plan.
The client is referred to the Financial Advisor for a cash-flow analysis.
Introduction is best made via email.

CHAPTER 10

Cash-flow analysis is reviewed by the Financial Advisor and client.
Values Ascertation: "Finding out what's really important."

CHAPTER 11

If loan is approved by underwriting a pre-approval letter is issued.
Search for property begins.
Make an offer.
Realtor refers Real Estate Attorney for Purchase & Sale review.
Schedule home inspection.

CHAPTER 12

Attorney reviews offer.
Attorney reviews their role in the process and the importance of the contigency dates and owner's title.

CHAPTER 13

Lender puts loan into process (appraisal and title are ordered and necessary documents are gathered) and re-consultation is scheduled to firm up the details of the loan structure.

Re-consultation: Details are firmed up regarding new property and desired loan structre. Communication is made with client's existing network to make sure the plan is aligned (referral is made to Property & Casualty Agent).

CHAPTER 14

Property & Casualty Agent reviews for proper homeowners coverage including the umbrella policy.

CHAPTER 15

A Special Closing Gift

Marc's team was so efficient that the appraisal happened earlier than expected, and actually took place on the same day as the inspection. As confident as Tom was, the road to closing was not a smooth one. The home inspection report revealed a few problems with the house. Chuck was right; there are no perfect inspections. He compared Chuck's notes to the report. He thought how great it was that Chuck took notes during the inspection so that he and Kim could really focus. Chuck's suggestion to get a babysitter also made a big difference. As it turned out, the deck was settling slightly and would need some reinforcement—in fact, the back railing had to be replaced entirely. And the hot water heater might need replacing sooner rather than later. Looking at the report, Tom's heart sank, but then he realized what he should do. He immediately went across the hall to show the report and Chuck's notes to John.

"Yeah, reading inspection reports is not fun," John said, rubbing his chin as he reviewed the pages. "But nothing here looks like a deal breaker. What were Chuck's thoughts? He'll be able to tell you how to proceed. But don't worry. You look as if you've got a fine house there."

As it turned out, Chuck was well ahead of Tom. He sent Tom an e-mail letting him know his thoughts on how to negotiate the repair of the railing, as well as some other items from the report. He received a copy of an e-mail from Chuck to Marc's team, letting them know that there were a few minor inspection issues to negotiate and that there could be a railing issue that the appraiser might comment on, and he asked if they needed to push back the commitment date.

"Uh oh," Tom said as he printed out the e-mail and showed it to Kim. She sat back, rubbing her very round pregnant belly, and sighed. "I knew it. We are going to lose the house all because of a stupid railing."

"I'll call Chuck. That can't happen, can it?" Tom was already dialing the phone. He got Chuck's voicemail and recorded his message.

"Hi Chuck, it's Tom. I just saw your e-mail to Amy Marie, and Kim and I are really worried about it. It's not a good thing to move the commitment date, is it? What's going to happen? Will this affect our deposit? What if the sellers refuse to fix the railing? Can they pull out now? Can you give us a call? Thanks."

Tom hung up the phone and was making Kim a cup of tea when the phone rang. "It's Chuck," he called to Kim when he saw the number on their caller ID.

"Hi Chuck," Tom said, hitting the speaker button on the phone. "What do we do now?"

"Take a deep breath and calm down," Chuck said in a very reassuring voice. "You have to remember that the sellers want to sell the house and move on with their lives. It is common for this to occur. Let me call the listing agent and advise her on these issues. Please let me know what else is important to you and Kim so I can negotiate a complete inspection repair/credit list. I'd rather you not have to spend any money until you actually own the house. The good thing is the listing agent was at the inspection, so she saw everything that I pointed out. The fact that the appraisal and inspection happened at the same time could turn out to be blessing in disguise. Since the appraiser commented on the railing, the lender will require the repairs to be completed. When listing agents are not engaged in the inspection, negotiations can get difficult. The seller is going to need to make the repairs prior to closing. That is reasonable."

"Okay," Tom said. "As long as we figure out a way to move forward and get the darn thing fixed."

"Yes," Kim said.

"All right," Chuck said. "I'll call the listing agent. Let's finalize our list today."

Later that afternoon, just as Tom was getting the boys ready for a trip to the playground, Chuck called again.

"We have good news," he said. "The seller has agreed to fix the railing, and drop the price for the value of the water heater and the other minor issues that concerned us."

"That's great, Chuck," Kim said. "How did you do that?"

"I have a contractor in my network who has agreed to do the work right away at a very fair price. I explained to the listing agent that the appraiser will want the railing repaired and that other potential buyers will ask for the same thing. Does that work for you?"

"Yes, that's great." Tom breathed a sigh of relief. He was very happy to have his Core 7 team watching out for his family and protecting him.

Still, as the closing day approached, Tom began to feel anxious again. He was worried that the final numbers would be higher than they expected and it would be too late to back out of the deal, as can happen when you get a car repair bill. He wondered if it was all too good to be true.

Tom walked into his office to find a voicemail message from Amy on Marc's team. "Please give me a call," she said. "I would like to go over your final numbers with you for the closing."

"Perfect timing," Tom thought. "Just when I was beginning to drive myself crazy."

He waited until he was at home with Kim before he returned the call. Amy faxed them the paperwork and walked them through every line on the final settlement statement. He did not expect this extra service and it came just in the nick of time.

"Thank you, Amy. We really appreciate this. It was a big help."

"Oh, we always call our clients to review the statement," she said. "I get a document called the Preliminary HUD-1 Settlement Statement the same day you do. I can review it with you to make sure it is correct before the attorney prepares the Final HUD-1 Settlement Statement, so don't panic if there is anything that doesn't look right. It can be very confusing, especially when it's your first time. Good luck with the closing."

As it turned out, they needed a little luck and then some. The night before the closing, Kim couldn't sleep. She kept shifting in bed trying to find a comfortable position, but her back ached. Her tossing and turning finally woke Tom as well.

"Are you all right?" he asked groggily.

"I can't sleep. I think I have to go to the bathroom. Maybe that will help."

She got out of bed, moaning softly as she padded her way across the carpet. Tom rolled over to go back to sleep but couldn't.

"Kim, are you okay?"

"Tom?" Her voice sounded very far away. "My water just broke."

Tom hopped out of bed and grabbed a sweatshirt. He knew from the delivery of their second child that Kim's labor could go a lot faster than it had with Tommy Jr. They couldn't waste any time, just in case.

Kim walked slowly out of the bathroom. "I'll get my things. Call John and ask him to come over and watch the boys."

It all happened so fast. Tom glanced at the hospital clock as he and Kim walked into the emergency room. It showed 4 a.m. By 6 a.m. Kim had given birth to a beautiful baby girl. They named her Lisa.

By 7:30 a.m., Kim was in her own room quietly nursing the new baby. She looked up at Tom. "What are we going to do about the closing?"

Tom fell into his chair with a thud and ran his fingers through his hair. He had forgotten all about the closing. "We'll have to reschedule," he said, shaking his head. "What else can we do? I'll call Chuck on his cell right now."

But once again—and Tom realized he should be used to it by then—Chuck surprised him.

"I'm glad you called so early," he said brightly. "I'll call your attorney and see if we'll be able to meet you at the hospital. Let's see if we can do the closing there at the same time we had planned."

"Are you serious? That's great! Will that really work?"

"Well, it's not as ideal as closing at the attorney's office," Chuck said with a chuckle. "But sometimes we have to jump through hoops to get things done. I'll call Josh now. And, Tom?"

"Yeah Chuck?"

"Congrats on the new baby!"

"Thanks."

Tom went back into Kim's room, rubbing his eyes in disbelief.

"What did he say?" Kim asked.

"He said we can still do the closing—here." Tom laughed.

"Can we really? Oh my god, I'm such a mess."

"No, it's okay. We're not doing it until the afternoon, at our original time. Here, I'll take the baby back to the nursery. You get some rest. I'll go home and take a shower and tell John and the boys what's going on."

Tom rocked the infant gently in his arms as he walked down the hall. "Hey little girl," he cooed. "You're going home soon." Then he realized something. Home would be different for Lisa than for the boys. The first and maybe only childhood home she would know would be their house. What would that be like for her? She would never know all the stuff they had gone through. But that was okay with Tom. "You're one lucky little girl," he said.

When Tom got back to the apartment, he found balloons tied to their doorknob.

"Congratulations!" He walked in to find John waiting there with Tommy Jr. and Ben. Tom grabbed the boys and hugged them.

"How's Mom and the new baby?" Tommy Jr. wanted to know.

"Both fine. You have a little sister and her name is Lisa. And guess what? By the end of the day we will own a house." He looked at John. "We're going to close at the hospital this afternoon."

"Yay!" the boys yelled, jumping up and down.

"Welcome to the world of homeowners," John said, shaking Tom's hand.

"We wouldn't have gotten here if it weren't for you," Tom said. "Thank you so much."

"Don't thank me yet," John said, an impish look in his eye. "Thank me later. Much later. This is just the beginning. Your financial planning doesn't end with the closing of this house."

That afternoon Tom was happy to see Kim refreshed by her nap and feeling as positive as he did about the closing. "Isn't it funny that we should feel so happy when we're about to sign our names agreeing to pay such a huge amount of money?" Kim mused.

"I think we can thank our Core 7 team for that," Tom said. "We feel good because we understand what we're doing and why we're doing it. We wouldn't be so well-informed if it weren't for them."

Someone knocked on the door. "Is someone talking about us?" Chuck said as he walked into the room. Josh followed and both greeted them warmly.

Josh began reviewing the documents with Tom and Kim and explained what they would be signing. "You have signed these before in your up-front disclosures," he said. "The big difference is these are official documents that are binding." The documents included:

- A promissory note promising to pay the loan and interest in full.
- The mortgage document which, Josh explained, secured the promissory note by giving the lender an interest in the property and the right to take and sell the property (foreclose) if the mortgage payments weren't made.
- A truth-in-lending form requiring the lender to reveal in advance the approximate annual percentage rate of the loan over the loan's term.
- A typed loan application form.
- A payment letter explaining the amount of their first payment and when it was due.
- An affidavit stating that Tom and Kim's various names (including Kim's maiden name) all referred to the same person.
- A survey form stating that Tom and Kim had seen a survey of the property and that it fairly depicted the property.

- A private mortgage insurance application, usually required on loans like theirs, with a down payment of less than 20 percent.
- A termite (or other inspection) form, indicating that Tom and Kim had seen a report of any inspections that were made.

When all of the documents and checks had been signed, Chuck handed Tom and Kim a large brown envelope. "Here are all the keys to the house, clearly marked," he said. "Congratulations, you're homeowners."

Chuck shook their hands and placed a large bottle of wine on Kim's bedside table. Tom didn't recognize the label at first, but then he realized it was a customized label—the image on it was a photo of their house. "Oh wow, thank you," Tom cried. He looked at Kim. She was looking at a card Chuck had handed her. "Here's to the beginning of your dream," it read. Kim had tears in her eyes as she leaned back against her pillows. "Chuck, we can't thank you—all of you—enough," Kim looked around the room at their team. "This has been an amazing learning experience. Thank you so much."

"Knock, knock, can anyone join this party?" Marc came in holding a small pink box tied with a white ribbon.

"Marc, what are you doing here? We just finished the closing," Tom said.

"Yes, I heard. Chuck told me what was going on. I just wanted to stop by with this little gift for the new baby and offer my congratulations." He handed the box to Kim and she unwrapped it. Inside was a tiny silver spoon.

"Oh, it's beautiful. Thank you."

"I thought it was the right thing," Marc said. "You're giving her a great start in life. This will remind her of that when she gets older."

As Marc and Kim chatted and Josh packed up his briefcase, Tom took Chuck aside. "This really all started with you," he told Chuck. "I'll happily refer my family and friends to you. But will we get to work with you again?"

"Oh, absolutely, I'm not going anywhere. A lot of people think they only need a realtor when they buy or sell a property, but I will always be a resource for you. Marc will do an annual mortgage review. I will do an annual equity assessment showing what the value of your home is, and Michael will coordinate with everyone to make sure your whole Core 7 team is communicating. I'll keep you up to speed with property values in your area and the changing real estate market. I can also be your advisor in helping you to assess whether making home improvements will improve your property value or not. When you need them, I can be a valuable resource to other professionals like roofers, electricians, plumbers, and landscapers."

"That would be great," Tom said.

"And don't forget your goals for investing in real estate in the future. I'm your expert in building a real estate portfolio. An agent who is an expert in assessing investment properties is incredibly rare and extremely valuable. My team and I take a lot of pride in knowing how to assess property and making sure the rental rates work in your favor to create an asset in your overall financial plan. We'll work up a *spreadsheet** that will help you see if the investment properties you look at make good financial sense."

"Yes, I'll definitely want to start thinking about that," Tom said.

"Well, you don't have to do it today. Enjoy your new house and your new baby."

---

* For a copy of the spreadsheet go to *www.whats-your-rate.com*

A few days later, as Tom was opening the bag of packing tape he had bought, the phone rang.

"Hey, Tom, it's Marc."

"Hi! I didn't expect to hear from you. Is everything okay with our mortgage?"

"Oh yes," Marc said. "That's not what I'm calling about. First of all, how are you and the new baby?"

"We're all fine here, excited about the move, of course. I'm just organizing stuff to start packing now."

"That's great. I know you will be very happy with the house. I'm calling because I wanted to do a brief closing survey with you. This is how I learn about how I'm doing and how I can get better. It's just a few questions, is that okay?"

"Sure."

"Okay. How did we do? How was the process for you?"

"Well, Kim and I were both happy with it. In fact, we were saying at the closing that we weren't nervous because you all did such a good job of explaining things to us."

"That's good to hear," Marc said. "Now, what can we improve?"

Tom had to think a moment about that one. "We liked the charts and other visuals you showed us. More of those wouldn't hurt. Numbers and figures can be mind-boggling. I like having another way of looking at the picture."

"I get it," said Marc. "Okay, that's it."

"Thank you, Marc, you've been great. I told Chuck we really could not have done this without all of you."

"You're welcome. It's what we do," Marc said. "Oh, by the way, if you know anyone who is interested in purchasing or refinancing a home, please call me with their name and number. I'd be happy to follow up with them for you."

"Yes, I'd be happy to do that," Tom said. "In fact, it would be a pleasure."

"Good. Well, that's it for now. You know that Michael, your financial planner, will be calling you in a few days, right?"

"Oh, yeah, that's right. I've been so busy I almost forgot."

"That's okay. Just make sure you make some time with him. You have a lot to discuss now."

"Will do. Thanks so much, Marc. Take care."

"You too. Good-bye, Tom."

Review

CHAPTER 6

Referral is given to realtor. The best introductions are made via email with both the Realtor and client copied.

CHAPTER 7

Realtor makes appointment at the office.
Buyer meeting at the Realtor's office.
Realtor refers the Mortgage Originator.

CHAPTER 8

Mortgage Originator sets an appointment with the client for a loan consultation. Pre-consultation worksheets are filled out prior to the consultation and analyzed by the Mortgage Originator.

CHAPTER 9

The Loan Consultation: The loan is integrated into the borrower's overall financial plan.
The client is referred to the Financial Advisor for a cash-flow analysis.
Introduction is best made via email.

CHAPTER 10

Cash-flow analysis is reviewed by the Financial Advisor and client.
Values Ascertation: "Finding out what's really important."

CHAPTER 11

If loan is approved by underwriting a pre-approval letter is issued.
Search for property begins.
Make an offer.
Realtor refers Real Estate Attorney for Purchase & Sale review.
Schedule home inspection.

CHAPTER 12

Attorney reviews offer.
Attorney reviews their role in the process and the importance of the contigency dates and owner's title.

CHAPTER 13

Lender puts loan into process (appraisal and title are ordered and necessary documents are gathered) and re-consultation is scheduled to firm up the details of the loan structure.

Re-consultation: Details are firmed up regarding new property and desired loan structre. Communication is made with client's existing network to make sure the plan is aligned (referral is made to Property & Casualty Agent).

CHAPTER 14

Property & Casualty Agent reviews for proper homeowners coverage including the umbrella policy.

CHAPTER 15

All loan approval conditions are satisfied (appraisal, income verification, etc.). Loan is approved.

The Closing! The final documents are signed.

The Financial Plan
Tying It All Together

The following week, still basking in the glow of closing on his house, Tom opened his e-mail to find a message from Michael, the financial advisor.

"Congratulations on the closing of your new home," the message read. *"It is probably the largest investment of your life, and we want to make sure we protect that asset. Let's make sure we put the right plan in place for it. I just wanted to check that we were still on for this week."*

Tom sighed. He had the urge to put Michael off and wait. He wanted to savor the moment of the close, plus they had already begun packing and planning the move. He didn't want to think about numbers anymore right now. But then he remembered how he had promised John to do exactly what the Core 7 team advised, that it's an ongoing process. And didn't John say this was just the beginning of the journey? It seemed silly to quit now.

He hit "reply" and told Michael he and Kim would be there for the appointment as scheduled.

"Please sit down," Michael said to them a few days later. "It's good to see you—and a smart decision on your part. A lot of people don't want to come in right after a closing. They want to take a break from the work of planning. But often they get busy moving into a new home and then life takes over, and they don't come back to it."

Tom looked at Kim and shifted uncomfortably in his seat. "Well, I'll admit I wasn't too excited about coming in. I thought about canceling. It seems that we've been through so much lately. A break would have been nice. But I promised someone that we wouldn't do this halfway, that we would listen to all of our Core 7 advisors."

"Good for you," Michael said. "Not moving on to this phase of planning is one of the biggest mistakes people make. This may be the most important part. You have to think of it like a car. If one of the four tires is out of balance—out of alignment—it will eventually affect the other three and possibly ruin the whole car. It's not something you do once and are done with it; it's a consistent, ongoing review as your life changes. It is so important in so many ways to do things as soon as possible and not as they are needed. Doing things sooner is always the best way."

"Yeah, best to just get it done," Tom said.

"Yes, but it really does make things better. One big reason for that is it is always cheaper. Think of insurance. The sooner you start buying it, the cheaper it will be because you are younger and healthier. Think of investing. The sooner you start investing, the sooner you get to take advantage of compounding interest. Think of your taxes. The sooner you have great tax advice, the sooner you keep more of your money in your pocket. Think about real estate investing, which I know you're interested in, Tom. The sooner you are able to buy real estate as an investment, the sooner you can start earning passive income with outstanding tax breaks. The sooner you have a real estate agent who understands investment property, the sooner you will find the best properties. Does this make sense?"

Tom and Kim both nodded. "I knew one or two of those examples," Kim said, "but I didn't know time could affect so many decisions."

"It works both ways," Michael noted. "Waiting to do something will have more of a detrimental effect on your outcome than you realize. Procrastination can be expensive. Let me give you an example: if a 30-year-old saves $100 a month up to the age of 65, and earns 10 percent per year, the resulting account would be worth $379,664. But if this person put investing off for just one year, beginning her savings at 31 instead of 30, her account at age 65 would be worth only $342,539. The cost of not saving $100 a month for just one year amounts to $37,125. Can you really afford to lose $37,125?"

"I don't think so," Tom replied. "Let's get to work. I'm going to feel that I'm losing money until we finish everything."

Michael laughed. "Great point. Little things done consistently over long periods of time can make a huge impact. Now, the first thing we want to discuss is how to tie some specific goals to your values, which we discussed in our first meeting. The most important thing, as I said earlier, is to align your values with your goals.

"Now, your first value is security. Security ties into all of your goals so that you can sleep at night. Now, to develop security, I always have my clients set up a reserve account, which I'm sure Marc also mentioned. The rule of thumb that I use is to have three months of expenses in a safe, liquid account for a base-salary, W-2 wage earner, and six months of expenses for a self-employed individual or a commissioned individual whose income varies and is inconsistent. I feel the self-employed need more reserves because of the potential of unforeseen events.

"You are a wage earner, Tom, but because security is one of your top values and so very important to you, I want you to strive for six months of reserves also. We want you to have a six-month cushion for all of your expenses if you are unable to earn income."

"Okay." Tom swallowed hard. Six months of expenses seemed like a lot of money. Could they really accumulate that? Tom then remembered and said, "Now I know why we didn't put the full 10 percent down on the house and kept it in savings."

"Exactly," Michael said. " I know you have goals that you have addressed with Chuck regarding purchasing real estate for investment income. Is that correct?"

"Yes," Tom replied. "Chuck helped us go through a worksheet that really breaks down the income we want, and the plan of purchasing an investment property. It is amazing how many benefits there are to owning real estate."

"Absolutely. Real estate is one of the best investments, if not *the* best. You are providing shelter for people, so the government gives you great tax breaks and incentives like depreciation and the ability to write off repairs. They also allow you to deduct the interest and taxes against the rental income you receive. Now keep in mind that the tax deduction for investment property works differently from owner-occupied property. The IRS only allows you to write off the interest and real estate taxes against the rental income, whereas on owner-occupied property, you can write it off against your earned income from your job. By the way, the accountant who will help you with your W-4 adjustments can get into the specifics when the time comes.

"With that being said, each time you purchase a rental unit, we want to adjust your cash reserves to cover expenses on that unit too. For example, if you buy a condo that costs you $1,000 a month for a payment, we want you to have six months of reserve, or $6,000, in a reserve account. We will also need to adjust your insurance needs to protect the asset, but we will discuss insurance later."

Condo Payment   = $1,000 per month

Reserves Needed = $3,000 for W-2,
Salaried Wage Earner

$6,000 for Self-Employed,
Commissioned or Bonus
Dependent
(or just conservative, cash reserves
are never a bad thing)

Tax Deductibility

Interest & Real Estate
Taxes on an
***Owner Occupied
Property***
= Deductible Against
your ***Earned*** Income

Interest & Real Estate
Taxes on an
Investment Property
= Deductible Against
the ***Rental*** Income
Only

Tom frowned. "Really? I'm not sure we can come up with that kind of money."

"You may not need six months of expenses," Michael assured him. "You may just need two to three months, but that would depend on your real estate agent's assessment of how easy it would be to rent the property. For example, if it's in an area where there are a lot of college students, it may be very easy to rent the property.

Fortunately, you are working with Chuck, who is the best in the business. You may only want to shoot for three months, to protect you from vacancy or if you need to fix the roof. As I said, it is an ongoing process."

"Okay, that makes sense," Tom said, nodding.

"Now, along with security, you mentioned that family is also important," Michael went on. "This also ties in with security and, as we mentioned, insurance and protection. I feel this is the foundation of a plan. Now let me explain about the three most important kinds of insurances you'll want to have that will give you security and protect your family. That is the main goal right, Tom and Kim?"

Tom and Kim nodded. They were both impressed with how well Michael understood their values and wanted to support them in maintaining them.

"The first is an umbrella policy. I'm sure that Marc told you about our famous athlete client when he recommended the property and casualty insurance agent during your home purchase. Am I correct?"

"Yes," said Tom. "At first I didn't know if we would ever have enough assets to consider needing an umbrella policy, but I'm beginning to see how our financial picture could quickly change."

Michael nodded. "You're right, Tom. The more you build up your assets, the more you need to protect them. Marc and I always bring up the fact that there is a 1-in-1200 chance that your home will burn down. And when you get a mortgage, every mortgage lender requires that you get fire insurance. However, you have a 1-in-200 chance of being sued, but very few people have an umbrella policy.

"Imagine this. I want you to think of yourself as being rich. You own a lot of property, you have retirement savings, and one of your children is 17 years old. He asks to take the family car to go out with his friends. You get a call a few hours later that he got into a car accident, and it was his fault. He was changing a song on the radio and when he looked up, he slammed into another car. Your child is fine, but the man he hit was a surgeon with a family, who now is unable to work and earn income in his current profession. There is a good chance that your homeowner's insurance policy will not cover all the liability, like repairing his car, medical expenses, damages the court may award from a potential lawsuit, and most importantly, his loss of income. In that case, the surgeon would sue you personally, but if you had an umbrella policy in place and were found liable, your assets would be protected. Such a policy only costs a few hundred dollars a year, and it can make all the difference in the world."

"Yes, that's what Marc and Phyllis, our insurance agent, told us," Tom said. "So we did get the umbrella policy when we purchased our homeowner's insurance." With that Tom was feeling grateful, and a little ahead of the game. It was comforting to know that this piece had been taken care of, and Phyllis had been really easy to work with.

"Good," Michael said. "The next insurance that we need to look at is disability insurance. Tom, let me ask you, what would you say is your greatest or most valuable asset?"

"Well," Tom said, looking at Kim, "I would say it is our house. I mean, we just put so much money into it. I would definitely say that's our most valuable asset."

"Good thinking," Michael said. "But the answer is actually your ability to work and produce income. What would you do if you were injured and could not work and earn income?"

"That would be disastrous," Tom said. "We would probably have to start using any reserves that we had."

"What if you were out of work for a long time and had to use up all your reserves?" Michael asked. "How would make your mortgage payment? Disability is one of the top causes of foreclosure in this country by far. You need both cash reserves and disability insurance. The disability insurance will replace your income while you are unable to work. However, there is usually a waiting period before the disability coverage kicks in, usually about ninety days, so you will need the cash reserves to cover your day to day living expenses and your mortgage and car payments until the waiting period is over. This will also protect your credit score. The last thing we want is for your credit score to drop. This would negatively affect your ability to refinance and the interest rates you obtain on home and auto loans, and it would cause a myriad of other financial ramifications.

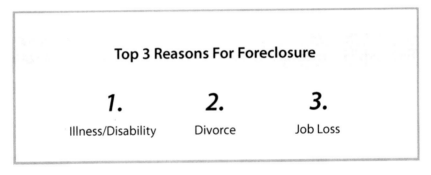

"Consider the doctor we talked about in the umbrella policy example. If this doctor has a really big income, we're talking about an awful lot of money that needs to be replaced. Tom, your income may not be that big right now, but I think we should get the best disability policy possible and we will always adjust it as your income increases. Disability is hard to qualify for sometimes, so it is best to get as much as you can at a young age while you are the healthiest. Does this make sense?"

"Yes, kind of like the sooner-rather-than-later discussion we had earlier, right?" Tom asked.

"It sounds like a disability policy would also keep me from being forced to go back to work if something happened to Tom. Is that right?" Kim asked.

"Yes, right on both counts," said Michael. "You obviously understand how important this kind of insurance is. We want you to be at home caring for your kids and maybe Tom as well, if he needs you.

"Okay, now let's talk about life insurance. It is definitely the most difficult topic to discuss but one of the most important. I have to ask you both a difficult question." He paused a moment, took a breath, and then looked directly into Tom and Kim's eyes.

"Kim and Tom, if one of you were to suddenly pass away, would you want your family to have an easier lifestyle, the same lifestyle, or a tougher one while mourning your loss?"

Tom and Kim looked at each other. They had never heard the question put in that way before. They knew very well what would happen if one of them died, but not specifically about how their family would live.

Tom cleared his throat. "Well," he began slowly. "I think myself or Kim would need a lot of time to mourn and be there for our children. I can't imagine trying to earn an income and worrying about our finances at a time like that."

"Yes," Kim said. "If Tom died, I'm not sure I would be able to focus on looking for work, or anything else for that matter." At that moment she turned to Tom and said, "Oh my god, who would take care of the kids while I was out looking for a job?"

"I'd want them to have a better life of course," Tom added. "I would hate to put a burden on my family at such a sad time."

"That is why life insurance is so important and why I ask about it in that way," Michael said. "This answer is almost always 'a better life.' The reason I do this is because people have so much difficulty thinking or talking about their own potential death. It's easier to focus on their family."

"It's not an easy discussion, that's for sure," Tom said.

"That's why so many people don't have it," Michael said. "When the World Trade Center towers in New York City went down during the terrorist attacks on 9/11, many of the people who died worked for prominent financial institutions and had considerably large incomes. But a number of their families struggled and had a difficult time keeping their homes. Do you know why?"

"No, why?" Kim asked.

"Because most of these financial professionals had no life insurance. None. When they were gone, their families had no way to replace the income. It added even more stress and sadness on top of what was already a terribly sad situation."

"That's just awful," Tom said, shaking his head.

"Well, a lot of people think of insurance in terms of replacing someone—that's what makes it so difficult to discuss. But it helps to remember that life insurance is not there to replace you. Nothing can do that. Life insurance replaces the income you earned."

"There are two kinds of life insurance—permanent insurance and term insurance. Both have positive and negative features, but for now, term is very good for you, but only because of its affordability. I feel very strongly that we should incorporate permanent insurance into your plan and there are significant tax and estate benefits of having cash value insurance. We will review this with your accountant and estate planning attorney."

"Well, for the purposes of our discussion now, what do you suggest?" Tom asked.

"My suggestion is we do a hybrid of term insurance and permanent life insurance with the option to convert the term insurance to cash value later on if necessary and if possible."

"Okay, that makes sense," Tom said.

"Now," Michael went on, "we want to make sure you protect each asset. For example, if you buy another property with Chuck, we need to increase your coverage to make sure the new property is covered. It is also very important to consider the cost of the insurance because those costs, along with the rates of return you will receive on your rental properties, must be factored into your real estate goals with Chuck."

"Yes, Chuck actually has that built into the *spreadsheet** that we filled out with him. It helps us figure out what we are looking for in returns," Tom said.

"Okay, that's good. Let me show you how that would work with real numbers. Let's say you need $1 million of life insurance in place to cover your mortgages and replace your lost income. Then you purchased a new property worth $300,000. We want to make sure that we increase your life insurance and umbrella policy limits to cover that new asset, so the new policy would need to cover $1.3 million. Does that make sense? The main factors in your situation that we need to cover are the ability to pay off all of your debt, maybe cover college expenses, and to replace any lost income to your family. The proper plan will protect your family so you can have the security and peace of mind that you'll be able to keep your family safe if you are not here anymore."

"Yes," Tom said, nodding. "One of my biggest fears in thinking of my death is worrying about my family struggling to make ends meet.

---

*   For a copy of the spreadsheet go to *www.whats-your-rate.com*

I had a dream about that and it was awful because there was nothing I could do about it. Now, doing this will give me so much peace to know that my family will be okay." Tom stopped and blinked. "You know what? Insurance is kind of like a safety net."

Michael smiled. "I think you're right, Tom. Beyond that, life insurance is also a great estate-planning tool to maximize your tax benefit. By the way, I am setting up a meeting with the accountant on my team for you to discuss adjusting your W-4 with your employer, so that you can receive more of your earnings on a monthly basis. That way, you won't have to wait until the end of the year to receive your tax benefit from the interest and taxes you're able to write off on your home loan. Also we are going to discuss your goal of starting a second business in the future. Nothing concrete, just some of the basics every person interested in starting a business should know. Our meetings with the accountant will become more frequent when you start your own business. The tax and business planning opportunities for the self-employed business owner are unlimited. A business owner especially needs the Core 7 team."

"You're already planning for my business?" Tom was stunned. Until now they had mentioned the business as a goal, but for him it really seemed like a dream.

Kim was thinking the same thing. "Can we really start a business now?" she asked.

"Well, you can start it whenever you like," Michael replied. "That's what this planning is all about. We're laying the foundation so you can get to work on the pieces you want to make happen first." Michael paused a moment. "Maybe now is a good time to ask how this whole conversation is making you both feel."

"I'm surprised I don't feel overwhelmed," Tom said. "I was stunned for a moment there when you mentioned the business, but now I'm starting to see that all the stuff we've been talking about can become real, not just dreams we'll always be chasing."

"Yes," Kim said. "It really feels good and comforting that we finally have a plan to move our family forward."

"Good," Mike said, nodding. "Now, let's get to retirement savings, which will address your desires to travel, spend a lot of time with your family, and have some fun and excitement." He paused again. "Before I forget, I just wanted to say you both have a really great list of values. They are connected with people and emotions. They're not about acquiring things just for the sake of having them. I see that all the time."

"Thank you," Kim and Tom said, smiling at each other. They liked having Michael's affirmation of ideas that meant so much to them.

"Okay," Michael went on, "we want to be able to invest 10 percent of your income for retirement. And believe me, you're going to need it. Tom, if you and Kim retire at 65 and live to a normal life expectancy of 83, you are going to eat 39,420 meals (three meals a day) over 18 years. If each of those meals costs $5, you would spend $197,100 on just food in retirement."

"Okay, now that's scary." Tom shook his head.

Michael went on. "The money you save can be placed in retirement accounts, mutual funds, or even real estate. The key is we have to be consistent. Let's make it automatic. When we make investing automatic, we get to take advantage of something called dollar-cost averaging. It means you invest the same amount, usually in something like a mutual fund, at the same intervals. This allows you to buy more shares when the price is low, and less shares when the price is high.

"Let me ask you this. Say you have $100 to invest each month, and in the first month, the investment costs $10 per share. In the second month, the price drops to $5 per share. What is your average price per share?"

"Well, I'd say $7.50 a share, right, Tom?" Kim said. "You just divide the $15 per share by two."

"Not quite," said Michael. He drew this chart for them on a sheet of paper:

Month	Amount Invested	Price per Share	# of Shares Purchased
1	$100	$10	10
2	$100	$5	20

= 30 shares for $200

"You have invested $200 dollars ($100/month) and you would have thirty shares in all because you bought ten shares in month one, but then you bought twenty shares in month two at $5 a share. That's $200 divided by thirty shares. So $6.67 is the average cost per share. That's the beauty of dollar-cost averaging. It forces you not to buy as many shares if the price goes up, and to buy more when the price goes down, thus giving you average lower costs.

"It's a good way to accumulate wealth and it gives you a greater chance to profit from your investments. The other great thing about dollar-cost averaging is you don't need a lot of money to get started. That means you can get started sooner rather than later. Remember our procrastination and caramel-macchiato conversation? The sooner we start investing, the sooner that money has time to grow."

"Can we really be that disciplined, though?" Tom wondered aloud.

"A lot of my clients have that worry. But if you take the money automatically out of a checking account before you get a chance to spend it, you don't really notice it. It's very easy to set that up with your bank investment company. The hard part—and this will require some discipline—is whenever you delete an expense, you want to move that money into an investment to increase your dollar-cost averaging. For example, if you pay off your car, refinance your mortgage, sell a property, get a raise at work or in any way increase your monthly cash flow, we need to adjust your automatic withdrawal to place that extra money into your dollar-cost averaging investment.

"I have a client whom Marc referred to me. Because of low mortgage rates and the opportunity to do multiple no-cost refinances, she has freed up over $500 a month in cash flow. Instead of that money going directly into her hands, so that she could spend it on something that isn't worthwhile, we reallocated the $500. It is taken directly from her checking account and has increased her dollar-cost averaging. That money can grow over time and make a big difference. Do you understand how quickly money like that can grow?"

	SUMMARY		
	Program Name	Original Loan	After the Refinances
	Loan Amount	$417,000	$417,000
	Interest Rate	6.5 %	4.5 %
1st Month	Term (months)	360	360
	Payment	$2,636	$2,113
	Mtg. Ins.	$0	$0
	Monthy Payment	$2,636	$2,113
	Net Savings	$0	$523

	IF THE SAVINGS WERE INVESTED	
	Program Name	After the Refinances
	Monthly Amount	$523
	Rate of Return	6%
After 15 Years	**Accum. Total**	$153,382
After 30 Years	**Accum. Total**	$528,511

$528,511! Wow! Those refinances were sure worth it...and it didn't cost me a dime!

Disclaimer: The 6% rate of return is an example, and is not guaranteed.

"I think I have a pretty good idea, but I couldn't tell you the exact numbers," Tom admitted.

Mike nodded again. "It grows quickly because of compound interest," he said. "In fact, Albert Einstein called compound interest, the eighth wonder of the world. I like to educate my clients to understand this better and be able to do some quick calculations themselves. Have you ever heard of the rule of 72?"

"No, we haven't," said Tom. "What does that mean?"

"The rule of 72," Mike explained, "is a way to figure out how long it will take for your money to double at a particular interest rate. All you have to do is divide the rate of return into 72. The result is the approximate number of years that it will take for your investment to double."

Law of 72

$10,000 @ 8% Return on Investment

The Investment will double in 9 years
(72 ÷ 8 = 9 years)

	Years	Balance
1	9.0	$20,000
2	18.0	$40,000
3	27.0	$80,000
4	36.0	$160,000
5	45.0	$320,000

"Okay, let me try this," Tom said slowly. "So, basically, if I have $10,000 in an investment that is returning 8 percent, I divide 8 into 72, which is 9. So, in nine years my investment will double and be worth $20,000, in 18 years it will be $40,000, and in 27 years it will be $80,000?"

Kim chimed in and said, smiling, "So in 36 years, the investment will be worth $160,000. I can see how the longer you keep your money invested, the more it grows."

"Yes, that is correct," Michael replied. "And don't forget, these numbers don't take into account any other investment contributions you make during that time. They are based on your original $10,000 investment. You see, financial planning has too many moving parts to manage on your own, or even to have just one professional managing it. You need a team. But, it is also very important for you to have a basic understanding of your investments and how they work, so that you can understand what the team is doing on your behalf."

"You're right," Tom said. "We know we are not experts, and a little knowledge can be dangerous." He and Kim laughed. "So we wouldn't make any moves without consulting our team of experts, but it helps to be able to understand it."

"Okay, so we are shooting for 70/10/10/10," Mike said. "That is 70 percent of your income to cover expenses; 10 percent going into conservative investments; 10 percent to be put aside for investments that yield higher returns like your real estate goals; and 10 percent should be for tithing and giving back. Trust me on this—giving back is a great thing to do. Right now you may not have the extra cash, but at least plan to give back. Even volunteering your time is a great thing."

"You'll have no argument there," Tom said. He was thinking of John's foundation and had already been thinking about how he could follow John's powerful example. "Kim and I understand how important it is to give back."

"So, just to recap," Mike said, looking at his notes, "we are going to be sure we maintain a six-month cushion for your cash reserves. You have purchased an umbrella policy to protect you if you are sued. We will submit the disability policy in case anything happens and you are unable to work. We are going to do a blend of permanent and term life insurance now, and when your cash flow is better, we can then discuss converting it all to cash value. By the way, a medical exam is needed for these policies. A nurse will contact you to schedule that appointment.

"For retirement, we are going to invest 10 percent into fairly conservative investments, and 10 percent into an account earmarked for higher returns, in your case, real estate. You are in great shape to buy investment property because you were conservative on your home purchase and didn't overspend. You have the discretionary cash flow to do this. In my experience, I have found the most common reason people don't reach their investment and retirement goals is because they overspend on their primary residence.

"Next, we will eventually set aside another 10 percent for charity and making a difference. I know we may not be there now, but we are going to work toward it. The important thing is that we are moving toward this goal. There are market cycles, good times, and bad times, but the key is that we stay focused on your goals and keep moving forward with them.

"To help you with that, we are going to constantly monitor your progress with a quarterly review, which we can do by phone."

"How long will that take?" Tom asked. He wasn't a big fan of long phone calls, and he couldn't see being on the phone for as long as it took to do this work today.

"Great question, Tom. If we are consistent and do them every quarter, many of these calls can just be five-minute check-in calls.

The problem comes when we don't stay in touch frequently. Then what happens is we only speak when there is a crisis or a major event. The calls or meetings can take much longer at that point. The key is for us to consistently do our reviews, monitor your progress, and keep your investments in line with your goals and values.

"Every time you make some cuts in spending or free up cash flow, we need to reallocate your savings and increase your investments. With every new purchase of investment property, we are going to adjust your protection needs and also account for that new income. So when you buy an investment property that earns a profit of $1,000 per month, we want to adjust for that income.

Does that all makes sense?"

"Yes, it sounds great." Tom and Kim agreed.

"Okay, now we have to plan for everything to be passed on correctly. I am going to bring you in to the estate planner, Terrie Smith. You'll speak with her about your goals concerning your children and their future. But we've been at this awhile. Why don't we take a break? Go to the bathroom, get some coffee. I'll meet you in the hall by my office in a few minutes and then I'll introduce you to Terrie."

"That's a great idea," Tom said, standing up. He relished the chance to stretch his legs. Planning for the future was hard work. "Taking a break will help us stay focused. I'm looking forward to talking to Terrie and I want to have my brain firing on all cylinders."

Review

CHAPTER 6

Referral is given to realtor. The best introductions are made via email with both the Realtor and client copied.

CHAPTER 7

Realtor makes appointment at the office.
Buyer meeting at the Realtor's office.
Realtor refers the Mortgage Originator.

CHAPTER 8

Mortgage Originator sets an appointment with the client for a loan consultation. Pre-consultation worksheets are filled out prior to the consultation and analyzed by the Mortgage Originator.

CHAPTER 9

The Loan Consultation: The loan is integrated into the borrower's overall financial plan.
The client is referred to the Financial Advisor for a cash-flow analysis.
Introduction is best made via email.

CHAPTER 10

Cash-flow analysis is reviewed by the Financial Advisor and client.
Values Ascertation: "Finding out what's really important."

CHAPTER 11

If loan is approved by underwriting a pre-approval letter is issued.
Search for property begins.
Make an offer.
Realtor refers Eeal Etate Attorney for Purchase & Sale review.
Schedule home inspection.

CHAPTER 12

Attorney reviews offer.
Attorney reviews their role in the process and the importance of the contigency dates and owner's title.

CHAPTER 13

Lender puts loan into process (appraisal and title are ordered and necessary documents are gathered) and re-consultation is scheduled to firm up the details of the loan structure.

Re-consultation: Details are firmed up regarding new property and desired loan structre. Communication is made with client's existing network to make sure the plan is aligned (referral is made to Property & Casualty Agent).

CHAPTER 14

Property & Casualty Agent reviews for proper homeowners coverage including the umbrella policy.

CHAPTER 15

All loan approval conditions are satisfied (appraisal, income verification, etc.). Loan is approved.

The Closing! The final documents are signed.

CHAPTER 16

Meeting with Financial Advisor to tie financial goals to the values set at the initial cash-flow meeting.

Introductions made to Estate Planning Attorney and Accountant to review legacy plan and tax plan with Financial Advisor.

CHAPTER 17

The Estate Planning Attorney

A Plan for When You Are Gone

Tom had been sincere with Michael. He was truly looking forward to meeting the estate planning attorney. As Michael led him and Kim down the hall to Terrie's office, he wondered if it was a bit premature. He felt he didn't really have anything to leave to his kids right then, other than their new home, so he didn't understand what they would be setting up. He had to fall back on his faith in John and his promise to follow the process and listen to all of his Core 7 advisors. He was sure Terrie, like the rest of his team, would explain it all.

"I am so glad to have the opportunity to work with you," Terrie said, shaking their hands as Michael introduced them. She took them to sit at a round mahogany table in the corner of her office. "Do you realize that just by being here, you're thinking in a way that the majority of the population can't or won't do?"

"Yes," Tom said as he looked at Kim and took her hand. "Michael told us that more than 50 percent of all people don't have wills in place. But I have to tell you, Terrie, I have been wondering, what good does a will do us right now? We don't have anything to leave anyone yet. Except our house."

Terrie smiled. "That's because you're thinking of wills as you've probably seen them portrayed on television or in the movies. You have a bunch of family members sitting around listening to this list of what they're going to get after some rich person has passed away. But a will is so much more—and therefore much more immediate— than that. Basically, a will gives you a voice when you're gone. For example, Janis Joplin left instructions that a portion of her estate be used for a party to be thrown in her honor after she was gone.

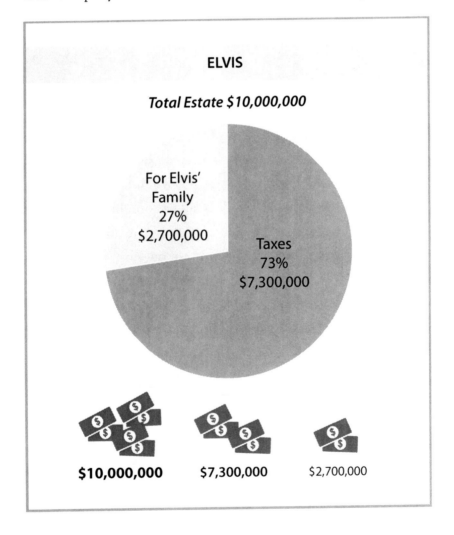

ELVIS

Total Estate $10,000,000

For Elvis' Family 27% $2,700,000

Taxes 73% $7,300,000

$10,000,000 $7,300,000 $2,700,000

Elvis Presley, on the other hand, had an estate in excess of $10 million and because there was no proper plan in place, his estate went through probate. Taxes and fees consumed a whopping 73 percent of the estate's value. Less than $3 million was left for his family, while the remainder went to estate taxes. And then there's the case of Marilyn Monroe's estate, which is still being contested in probate court because she didn't have a plan. Let me ask you a question. If you both walked out of here this afternoon and had a fatal car accident, who would have custody of your children?"

Tom and Kim looked at each other. They had just assumed Kim's extended family, her cousins, would look after the boys and they said so.

"Is it written down anywhere that they would be your children's guardians?"

"Well, no," Kim admitted. "We just thought they would come and take care of them."

"That doesn't happen automatically," Terrie said. "If you die without a will, your children become wards of the probate court. It would be up to the court to decide who would be their guardians. Now it's highly likely they would choose your family, Kim, but that wouldn't stop another family member from making a claim to them, particularly if there were assets involved, and the court would have to review such a claim."

"Why won't the court do what's right?" Tom asked.

"The court's view may be different. Remember, the court knows nothing about your family history or your wishes. The court will try to make the best decision for the kids based on the information being presented to them at that time. I've seen kids uprooted from their schools, even siblings separated, because there were no plans for their care after losing their parents. It's sad because it just adds to the grief they're already feeling."

"I almost can't bear to think of that," Kim said.

"Well, that's kind of the problem," Terrie pointed out, "most people don't want to think about it. Then tragedy happens and it's too late. You're doing the best thing you can for your children right now in thinking about how to take care of them."

She went on, "The will would cover you as well. What if you were injured and couldn't make decisions for yourself? A living will, or a healthcare proxy, tells the authorities how you want certain situations handled. For example, would you want to be kept on life-support indefinitely, or is there a certain time frame you would want your family, with the advice of your doctors of course, to decide there is no hope? You would also want a durable power of attorney, so the person you designate to act for you has the legal authority to do so."

Now Tom was really glad he had asked his question upfront. He saw more than ever the importance of having a will in addition to the rest of the planning they would do. "I do see the value in doing this work now. Thank you, Terrie."

"You're welcome, but you should know that the rest of your question is valid as well. You don't have much to leave anyone right now, but that situation is going to change as you get older and your finances grow. What we do today won't be set in stone. Estate planning, like every aspect of your financial well-being, is an ongoing process, not an event. Your circumstances will change so your plans must change too when that happens. You have to tune up your plan just as you would regularly tune up your car."

That made sense to Tom. After all, a couple of months ago he didn't own a house. Now he did and he knew he had to take steps to protect it.

"Michael will collaborate with me when changes occur to make the necessary adjustments. The more your life changes, the more we need to adjust. Ideally, I would do this every time you have a child, refinance or acquire another property, or receive an inheritance or windfall. The more you have, the more you need to plan. Also, I know from your work with Michael that legacy is important to you," Terrie said.

"Yes," Tom said. "I know I'm no Rockefeller, but I'd like to make a difference and help future generations of my family long after I'm gone. I want to help my grandchildren, and maybe even their grandchildren. I want to create a legacy and give my family and my future family a better life."

"That's a wonderful goal to have," Terrie said. "For that reason, we'll focus on both short-term and long-term estate planning. The short term will involve tools such as your will, healthcare proxy, and a durable power of attorney to cover your family now. For the long term, we'll talk about what it means to set up trusts, and how you can fund them for your legacy planning. Does that sound good to you?"

It was exactly what Tom wanted to hear.

At the end of the meeting with Terrie, Tom and Kim were surprised when she told them Michael wanted to see them before they left.

"Really?" Tom asked. "I thought we were done?" He had already been thinking about heading home and savoring the accomplishments of the day.

"It won't take long. Just a few details he wants to finish up," Terrie said.

Michael reiterated what Terrie had said. "Just a couple of things, starting with this question: Have you had a chance to think of that ultimate goal that we discussed in our original values conversation?

I know dreaming of something bigger now may seem impossible to obtain, given what we've already planned for, but I feel it's important that my clients dream a little bit and use their imagination to think about what would be perfect. You'll be surprised by what you can accomplish."

Tom looked at Kim and shifted in his seat. He was a little embarrassed that he had no definite answer for Michael. "I have been thinking about this, and I want to give back, and do something good for society. I'd like to make a difference, but it's hard for me to believe that anything we do can have that much of an impact."

"Tom, even if you only impact the lives of a few people, it's great. Think about it in those terms and maybe something will come to you. We can talk about that again later in another meeting.

"Now, one last thing—college planning is usually the last thing I discuss with my clients because I want to make sure that all of their other financial aspects are covered first. The reason is because your children can take loans out and finance college. When you pass away, as you've learned from Terrie, the rest of your assets will typically be passed on to them anyway, so you are better off building your retirement and other assets first. I've seen far too many people neglect their own retirement to fund their children's college education. I know that you don't want your children to have the financial burden of student loans as they are trying to get started in life, but you do want them to learn how to support themselves financially. Is that right?"

"Yes," Kim said. Tom nodded his agreement.

"College can be very expensive," Mike explained. "I follow a guideline called the 250/650/850 rule, which means that when a child is born, it will take $250 a month, until the child is 18, to invest in a fund to pay for a public college. To pay for a private college, it will cost approximately $650 a month for the 18 years. It will cost approximately $850 a month for 18 years to send your child to Harvard or another Ivy League school. According to the College Board, a college education for a baby born in 2010 will exceed $250,000 for an in-state school and will be more than $500,000 for a private college. These numbers are generalizations but are a fairly accurate assessment."

250/650/850 Rule

PUBLIC COLLEGE	$250 per month
PRIVATE COLLEGE	$650 per month
IVY LEAGUE	$850 per month

College

Cost of a 4 Year College Degree
2010-2014

Penn State*	$159,525
Maryland	$163,672
Berkeley*	$144,584
Notre Dame	$224,419
Harvard	$227,430
Georgetown	$216,439
Princeton	$221,443
Yale	$221,137

assumes 6% annual increase in the
cost of tuition, room & board based
on 2009-2010 prices
*out of state tuition

"Okay, that's depressing," Tom said.

"Yeah," Kim said, "that makes me feel that we're way behind. We definitely haven't saved that much for the boys and we haven't started anything yet for baby Lisa."

"It's all right," Michael said. "Remember, better late than never. What I recommend is we start allocating some extra cash toward a college fund such as the 529 plan. That allows you to save for college and enjoy certain tax benefits. After we satisfy your other goals, such as building your retirement and real estate portfolio, we can put more focus on building a college fund. Does this make sense?"

"Absolutely," Tom said, breathing a sigh of relief. It was amazing how much easier things were with someone like Michael showing the way.

"Now I want to quickly address your goal of a second home," Michael said. "I think a second home is a great place to relax and create memories with your family. I just want you to understand that a second home should not be considered an investment. It often means more money going out, in the form of another mortgage payment and all the expenses that go along with maintaining a second home. I'm not saying you can never have a second home, but everything in your investment plan needs to be done in the right sequence. Let's make sure we are way ahead in your investment plan before you buy the second home. If you buy it before that, you may want to consider renting it out to offset the expense. It would be better to wait until the time is right, though. We don't want to add any obstacles to the plan. Does that make sense?"

"Sure," Tom said, not sure he would be ready to jump into another home buying process soon anyway.

"Well, I think this is a good place to wrap things up," Michael said, getting up from his seat and walking over to his credenza. He turned and handed them a gift-wrapped box. Inside was a matted and framed list of Tom and Kim's values and goals, beautifully printed out as affirmations.

"I want you to read those every day," Michael said. "If you read them every day, you'll be more likely to stay focused on them and make them come true."

"Wow, thank you so much," Kim said. "I've never had anything like this before."

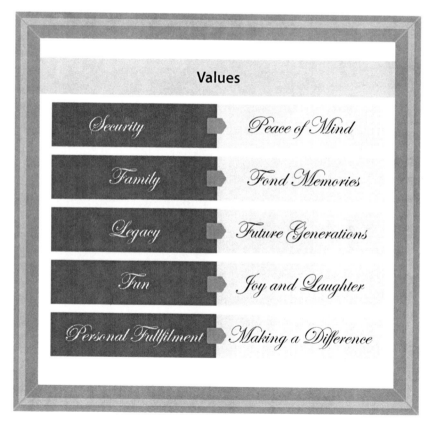

Tom said, "Now I'm beginning to see how all these things can actually happen. Thank you, Michael. As a matter of fact, we can't thank you enough. This has been an amazing day of work."

That night Tom and Kim invited John over for dinner and told him of the work they had done with Michael and Terrie.

"Yeah, Michael and Terrie are two of the best people out there," John said. "I trust them implicitly. They know their stuff. And they are definitely right; things just get more complicated as you get older. You have more stuff to plan for. It's really great that you've starting out doing all of this now. Can you imagine if you were starting from scratch like this twenty years from now?"

Tom groaned. "That would be a nightmare."

"Yes," Kim said. "And Tom has had that nightmare. He'll tell you that he's been there, done that."

Everyone laughed.

"You know, it's interesting how many people don't have a Core 7 team in place," Tom said. "I'm sure it's the reason so many people have financial troubles. It should be a requirement for every family to have a Core 7 team so they will have a good solid financial foundation."

"Maybe you can start a Core 7 foundation," Kim said with a giggle.

"That wouldn't be such a bad idea," John said. "Sounds like the kind of big goal you would have discussed with Michael."

"Actually we had a hard time with that one," Tom said. "Kim and I are still thinking about it. We just don't see how we can make such a big difference. Look at you, John, you started a whole foundation that will help a lot of people who get sick."

"You don't have to start your own foundation," John said. "There are other ways to leave legacies. Did Mike talk to you about cash value life insurance policies?"

"Yes, some cash value insurance is part of our plan," Tom said.

"The next time you talk to Mike, ask him about getting a policy as part of your giving back plan. You see, Tom, you could write checks and make charitable donations to an organization you care about, but what would happen after your death?"

"The donations would stop," Tom replied.

"Exactly, and the organization would only be able to receive the amount you've given them up to that point. Instead, you can set up a cash value life insurance policy with the charity named as the beneficiary and contribute the same amount. When you pass away, even if it is an early death, the death benefit and cash value that's been earning interest will go to the charity and they would get more than you could have possibly contributed in regular donations during your lifetime.

"I've had Michael in to speak to the whole board of directors at my foundation, as well as to our major donors, about this plan. The donors thought it was fantastic and picked up on it right away. Sadly, we experienced the effectiveness of the plan too soon. One of our members, who had been very active in the foundation, was tragically killed in a car accident. Her policy left a huge benefit to the foundation. With the money, we were able to start a whole new DNA research initiative in her name."

Tom crossed his arms and leaned back in his chair. "That's some story, John. You've definitely got me thinking. I'm seeing now that Kim and I can think about this big goal a little differently."

"Yes," Kim said. "We've been thinking we have to do something that's a big, grand gesture. Now we see that doing a little bit over time can have the same—or maybe even a bigger effect."

"That's right," John said. "All you have to do is figure out where you want to direct your focus."

"Thank you again," Tom said. "We owe you so much. We've learned so much from you. We can't thank you enough."

"You don't have to thank me," John said. "Just keep listening to your Core 7 team. Let's have a toast, shall we? Here's to making a difference."

"Yes," Tom said. "Here's to making a difference."

Review

CHAPTER 6

Referral is given to realtor. The best introductions are made via email with both the Realtor and client copied.

CHAPTER 7

Realtor makes appointment at the office.
Buyer meeting at the Realtor's office.
Realtor refers the Mortgage Originator.

CHAPTER 8

Mortgage Originator sets an appointment with the client for a loan consultation. Pre-consultation worksheets are filled out prior to the consultation and analyzed by the Mortgage Originator.

CHAPTER 9

The Loan Consultation: The loan is integrated into the borrower's overall financial plan.
The client is referred to the Financial Advisor for a cash-flow analysis.
Introduction is best made via email.

CHAPTER 10

Cash-flow analysis is reviewed by the Financial Advisor and client.
Values Ascertation: "Finding out what's really important."

CHAPTER 11

If loan is approved by underwriting a pre-approval letter is issued.
Search for property begins.
Make an offer.
Realtor refers Real Estate Attorney for Purchase & Sale review.
Schedule home inspection.

CHAPTER 12

Attorney reviews offer.
Attorney reviews their role in the process and the importance of the contingency dates and owner's title.

CHAPTER 13

Lender puts loan into process (appraisal and title are ordered and necessary documents are gathered) and re-consultation is scheduled to firm up the details of the loan structure.

Re-consultation: Details are firmed up regarding new property and desired loan structre. Communication is made with client's existing network to make sure the plan is aligned (referral is made to Property & Casualty Agent).

CHAPTER 14

Property & Casualty Agent reviews for proper homeowners coverage including the umbrella policy.

CHAPTER 15

All loan approval conditions are satisfied (appraisal, income verification, etc.). Loan is approved.

The Closing! The final documents are signed.

CHAPTER 16

Meeting with Financial Advisor to tie financial goals to the values set at the initial cash-flow meeting.

Introductions made to Estate Planning Attorney and Accountant to review legacy plan and tax plan with Financial Advisor.

CHAPTER 17

Estate Planner creates estate plan. Legacy plan is tied to goals and values.

CHAPTER 18

The Accountant

"What are you smiling about?" Kim asked as they walked across the parking lot to the office of their new accountant, Stephen Cohen. "Is it because we're finally meeting the last of our Core 7 advisers?"

"That's part of it." Tom laughed as he took Kim's hand. "I was just thinking that at least with this one, I actually know what he does already."

Kim laughed too and added, "You know, I've enjoyed doing all of this together."

Tom kissed her hand as they walked through the door. "Me too, honey. Me too."

Stephen turned out to be the oldest of their Core 7 advisors. He had perfectly trimmed white hair, but he seemed many years younger than their neighbor, John. Tom was thinking if he had to guess, he would assume Stephen was in his 50s.

"You know, Stephen, I was just telling Kim that out of all of my Core 7 advisors, yours was the job we felt we knew most about up-front. But can you tell me a little about how you fit in with the rest of the team in terms of what you do?"

"Certainly, Tom. I know it can be confusing because many accountants also act as personal advisors. They help manage assets and investments, plan for retirement and reduce your exposure to risk," Stephen explained. "However, I prepare and monitor your financial statements exclusively. "

"I see," Tom said. "Again, you guys are working in ways that make perfect sense."

"Yes, and I do fit in the picture well. I will have access to all of the work you continue to do with Michael, Marc, and the rest of your team. I'll help you make adjustments when any of it has an effect on your tax situation. As you acquire additional assets, your tax burden will become more complicated, as well as advantageous. For example, I'm sure Marc and Michael told you that we will look into reducing your withholdings, now that you've closed on your house. You'll increase your take home pay as a result."

Tom nodded, "I do remember that."

"So anything that you do that has tax implications, I'll be on top of it. And here, I wanted to give you this." He slid a sheet of paper over to them.

"This is a list of the documentation I'll need to see from you each year when it's time to prepare your taxes. A lot of my clients use that sheet to set up their filing system so they can put things in the right place all year long. I see fewer shoeboxes stuffed with receipts that way, but I would also understand if that's all you can get to me. Not everyone can be so organized."

"Oh, we'll be happy to get that organized," Kim said. "I'm just relieved that you're taking it off our plate. Doing taxes was not one of my favorite things."

"I'm happy to be of service." Stephen laughed. "You'll also see on that sheet a list of events you'll want to alert me to when they take place. For instance, you just had another child, right?"

Kim smiled. "Yes."

"Congratulations! Now I know we'll be declaring another dependent on your taxes. The team will usually keep everyone in the loop, but you should know that the more information we have, the more helpful we can be in advising you."

"Is there anything else you need from us right now?" Tom asked.

"No, the rest we can cover when it gets closer to tax time. Michael will get me the cost-basis of all of your investments, which helps me a great deal in figuring out your tax liability. The cost basis is the original price of an asset adjusted for things like depreciation, stock splits, and frequent buying and selling of the same asset, as with most mutual funds. It can get very complicated and the fact that Michael tracks this for all of his clients makes my job so much easier. Michael obtains this information from every new client he works with, even if they were working with another advisor, which, by the way, is something that not all financial advisors do.

"As you build your investment real estate portfolio, you will have great write offs, like depreciation, but keep in mind that with depreciation, the government is basically giving you a loan. Each dollar you write off as depreciation and pay less in taxes for, also lowers your cost basis. This means when you sell, you will pay a larger capital gains tax. Chuck and Josh can show you how to defer the capital gains tax through a vehicle called a 1031 exchange when that time comes. For now, though, you'll be getting many tax breaks because of your home purchase. I think you'll be really happy with the results."

"No, you're wrong," Tom said. "I'm already really happy with the results. This has been an amazing process."

Review

CHAPTER 6

Referral is given to Realtor. The best introductions are made via email with both the Realtor and client copied.

CHAPTER 7

Realtor makes appointment at the office.
Buyer meeting at the Realtor's office.
Realtor refers the Mortgage Originator.

CHAPTER 8

Mortgage Originator sets an appointment with the client for a loan consultation. Pre-consultation worksheets are filled out prior to the consultation and analyzed by the Mortgage Originator.

CHAPTER 9

The Loan Consultation: The loan is integrated into the borrower's overall financial plan.
The client is referred to the Financial Advisor for a cash-flow analysis.
Introduction is best made via email.

CHAPTER 10

Cash-flow analysis is reviewed by the Financial Advisor and client.
Values Ascertation: "Finding out what's really important."

CHAPTER 11

If loan is approved by underwriting a pre-approval letter is issued.
Search for property begins.
Make an offer.
Realtor refers Real Estate Attorney for Purchase & Sale review.
Schedule home inspection.

CHAPTER 12

Attorney reviews offer.
Attorney reviews their role in the process and the importance of the contigency dates and owner's title.

CHAPTER 13

Lender puts loan into process (appraisal and title are ordered and necessary documents are gathered) and re-consultation is scheduled to firm up the details of the loan structure.

Re-consultation: Details are firmed up regarding new property and desired loan structre. Communication is made with client's existing network to make sure the plan is aligned (referral is made to Property & Casualty Agent).

CHAPTER 14

Property & Casualty Agent reviews for proper homeowners coverage including the umbrella policy.

CHAPTER 15

All loan approval conditions are satisfied (appraisal, income verification, etc.). Loan is approved.

The Closing! The final documents are signed.

CHAPTER 16

Meeting with Financial Advisor to tie financial goals to the values set at the initial cash-flow meeting.

Introductions made to Estate Planning Attorney and Accountant to review legacy plan and tax plan with Financial Advisor.

CHAPTER 17

Estate Planner creates estate plan. Legacy plan is tied to goals and values.

CHAPTER 18

Meeting with Accountant to review possible adjustments to W-4 witholdings, future tax planning and financial integration.

CHAPTER 19

Gratitude

The sun shone bright and warm on the Saturday that Tom, Kim and their children moved into their new house. Though it seemed the unpacking would go on forever, Tom was amazed by how quickly they all settled into the house. It was as if they had lived there their whole lives. Tommy Jr. and Ben rode their bikes around and around the cul-de-sac circle every day after school. Tom would sometimes come home and find them sitting in the little fort section of the swing set, pretending to be pirates planning their next voyage.

Kim was enjoying nursing their baby daughter through infancy in the new house. The master bathroom featured a large tub—a luxury they didn't have at their old apartment. She loved ending a long day of unpacking boxes with a soaking bubble bath.

Tom discovered his favorite part of the house was the deck, especially when the summer days arrived. He would wake up before the rest of the family and sit out there drinking his coffee and enjoying the quiet and the fresh morning air.

One afternoon, Tom was sitting on his deck when his cell phone rang. He couldn't be more surprised by the voice he heard on the other end.

"Gwendolyn Davis here," she said. "How have you and Karen been?"

"Uh, you mean my wife, Kim? We're fine."

"That's good to hear. I was calling because I have a house that just came on the market very similar to the one you looked at with me. If you're still in the market, I'd love to show it to you. I know how much you wanted to get your family into a house."

"Yeah we did, and we have," Tom said. "We've had our home for several months now."

"Oh!" She hesitated. "Well, I guess congratulations are in order."

"Yes, thank you, Ms. Davis. See you around." Tom hung up the phone and couldn't help but have a good laugh at her expense.

He found himself feeling just as he had when he first learned Kim was pregnant: rich and bursting with gratitude. He was especially thankful for John and his guidance in leading him to his Core 7 advisors. Tom had recently referred one of his coworkers to Chuck with the same piece of advice John had given him. "You're going to work with an entire team," Tom told him. "Listen to them. It'll be the best thing you ever did."

It was the truth. Tom knew he would always refer people to Chuck, Marc, and everyone else on his team. He understood and appreciated the huge benefit of knowing that all of his advisors were communicating. Tom thought having to deal with so many names and faces during the purchase of his home would be daunting, but the Core 7 had made it so easy for him and Kim. He was deeply grateful for the peace of mind that told him all of his goals were going to be met. How could they not be? He believed he had the best advice—and the greatest advisors—in the world.

CHAPTER 20

Legacy

The Plan Comes to Fruition

The years passed and during that time all the things one would expect to happen happened: the children grew up, Tom and Kim retired and grew old. They moved to a condo in Florida that they had purchased years earlier as an investment property, with the help of a top agent in Florida whom Chuck had referred them to through his vast network across the country. They gave the family house they had purchased all those years ago to Lisa. It made sense. Her birth had started them on the journey to the house. Tom figured it would go to her for her family.

Then, many years later, the thing Tom once dreaded finally happened. He passed away. Tom Jr., Ben, and Lisa told their mother they would handle everything.

"Let us do this for him, Mom," Tom Jr. said. "It's the last best thing we can do for him."

The church was full for Tom's funeral. It was obvious from looking around the room that he had lived a full life with many people in it. As the music began, everyone rose to sing a hymn and Tom's casket was carried into the church. Behind it walked Kim, Tom Jr., Ben, and Lisa.

There wasn't a dry eye in the house. Everyone could sense the spirit of joy and gratitude at having known this great man. Nothing relayed that more than the moment when Tom's three children went up together to deliver the eulogy.

"Our father was a great man," Tom Jr. said, "and he made our lives great through his thoughtful, attentive, joyful approach to life."

They went on to tell stories of the wonderful memories they had of going to Disney World with their father, and of traveling over the holidays to see friends and relatives, all of whom filled the church at that moment. Lisa talked about choosing her husband because he was a family man just like her dad.

"And the greatest memory of my life is walking down the aisle with him at my wedding," she said, the tears welling up in her eyes. "He told me he didn't mind paying for the wedding because he knew I would remember that moment for the rest of my life and that memory would be priceless. He was right."

When Ben spoke, he talked about how his father told him he'd have to figure out how to pay for his own education. "At first, I was angry with him about it, but I realized I had to trust my dad. He never did anything without a reason. I worked my way through school and took out student loans. After I got my first job and made payments on the loans for a year, he told me he had a late graduation gift for me." The young man laughed and wiped tears from his eyes. "He had paid off my student loans."

"Our father wanted us to learn what he didn't learn until well into his adulthood," Tom Jr. said. "He wanted us to understand our finances. And once we did, he lovingly shared with us everything that he was doing. We learned how to manage his investment properties. In doing so, he was able to free himself up to work on the board of the John Randle Foundation, which he enjoyed doing until his dying day. But he was also giving us a tremendous opportunity because Ben and I got so good at managing properties, that we were able to start our own business doing it for other people. Our gratitude for our father has no boundaries. It is limitless."

Later, in Terrie's office, Tom and Kim's longtime estate attorney, the family began the process of reviewing Tom's will and estate. Tom's children couldn't believe the extent of the interests controlled by this simple man. Terrie described a bewildering array of properties, investments, assets, and trusts. Some things, such as certain real estate investments, were left specifically to one or more of his children. Other parts where donated to charities and cultural arts programs that had been close to Tom's heart, like the John Randle Foundation. Kim, of course, was the main beneficiary of the estate. She would be taken care of for the rest of her life.

Then Terrie described the last set of trusts, which surprised everyone. Tom had requested a series of trusts be set up for his future grandchildren. They would come into the money at the age of twenty-five, but only if they could prove financial stability, illustrated by a plan developed with a team of Core 7 professionals that included a realtor, a mortgage originator, a real estate attorney, a financial advisor, a property and casualty insurance agent, an accountant, and an estate planning attorney.

Tom's family was shocked, but incredibly grateful and happy. They hugged each other and laughed through their tears. "Where would we all be without Dad?" Ben asked his mother. "He's taken care of us and of our children."

"Mine too," Lisa piped in. "And I don't even have any kids yet. How incredible is that?"

"Not so much when you think about everything we've taught you over the years," Kim said quietly. "You're getting the benefit

Dad never had because we were so new to financial planning. You're getting to see how focus and planning pays off. You can do the exact same thing for your children and grandchildren. Just keep listening to your Core 7 team, and following the path your father and I laid out for you."

Tom Jr. nodded. "I'm overdue for my quarterly review with my financial guy," he said. "I'm going to call him when I get home and make an appointment."

"I'd like to get involved with the John Randle Foundation," Ben said. "It's time I started giving back. I've been so busy at work, I've let stuff like that fall by the wayside."

"Your father would have appreciated that," Kim said. "John Randle is the reason we have so much today. He got us started. He was the one who told us about having a Core 7 team."

"Jack and I started working on our list of values, but we never finished it," Lisa said quietly, looking over her shoulder at her husband. "I think it's time we got serious about it and finished it."

"All of those things are fine," Kim said. "But children, please remember this: do the things that mean the most to you. That's what all this work is about—figuring out your values, deciding how to give back, raising a family, building a home and your investments. You don't have to do exactly what we did. Having your own Core 7 team will help you live the life you want to live. If you can do that, the legacy your father left you will have the most meaning of all." She slowly rose from her chair. "Now, are we ready?"

"Yes, Mom," Ben said. "They're waiting for us. Let's go."

The late afternoon sun was low on the horizon as they pulled into the parking lot of the playground they had loved as children. Tom Jr.'s daughter and Ben's son were waiting for them with their mothers. They all held several brightly colored helium balloons. The children had written, "Thank you, Grandpa" on each one.

"We're ready, Grandma," they called out as Kim, holding Ben's arm, joined them with everyone else.

"Okay," she said. "Everyone take a balloon. Now gather around."

Kim took a blue balloon and held it in both of her hands. She kissed the top of it and whispered, "Thank you, my love. I'll see you soon." She opened her hands and the balloon floated away.

Everyone else released the rest of the balloons.

"Thanks, Dad!"

"Thank you, Grandpa. We miss you!"

"Thank you, Daddy."

The balloons lifted up toward the brilliant blue sky and grew tinier as they disappeared into the distance.

Acknowledgments

The author would like to thank:

Mom, Dad, Paula, Gina, Dominic, Valentina, Sophfronia Scott, Chuck Silverston, William Tatosky, Michael Moran, Justin Berke, Bill and Julie Brady, Brad Hartz, Nik Ligris, Kostas Ligris, Tammy Macherides, Michael Crotty, Lou Posner, Edward Gourdeau, Sharon Dostie, Josh Ribner, Jonathan Norris, Michelle Mazzella, Kimberly Etchings, David Jensen, Rick St. Jean, Greg Anderson, Angie Baker, Mariana Swanson, Marc Destfano, Erik Santucci, the DeNucci Family, Bard Conn, Lucien McPherson, Brian Anger, Bill McHugh, Jay McHugh, Tim Braheem, Khai Mcbride, Todd Duncan, Brian Buffini, Barry Habib, Jim McMahan, Sue Woodard, Brian Koss, Dana Rosenblatt, Paul Buonopane, Amy Dirazonian, Greg Delue, Eric Abenaim, Jason Luck, Fred Lipsius, Martha Harvey, Ron Gardiner, Steve Gaziano, Eric Steenstra, Kevin McGoff, Evan Kushner, Yitz Magence, Steve Marshall, Douglas Andrew, Nick Pasquerosa, Michael Sacco, the Santucci Family, Duncan and Kara Stewart, the D'Antonio Family, the Spezzano Family, the Murphy Family, Jim and Jen O'Connell, the Devasto Family, the Caddell Family, the Gordon Family, Jon Ufland, Holly Christiansen, Bowen School, Charles E. Brown Junior High School, Newton South and Newton North High School, the Newton Boys and Girls Club, the DeMaio Family, the Foley Family, Matthew and Dana Malone, Richard and Stephanie Maloney, Scott and Wendy Lennon, Chris and Sharon Nash, the Spagnoulo Family, the Hynds Family, the Rohanna Family, the Grinley Family, the Fontano Family, the DeSantis Family, the Freeman Family, John Maxwell, Ken Blanchard, Bob Burg, Robert Kiyosaki, Jim Comosa, the Trudo Family, the Belmonte Family, James Maiocca, Joan Sullivan, Stanley Kinzelburg, the Marini Family, Jon Gordon, Jim and Linda Morando, the Busa Family, the Riffe Family, Marc Gagaro, Nico Gagaro, the Sacco Family, Kevin Fox (and A+), Paul Shea, Doug Perry, Doug Gage, Dan Wilson, the Asaley Family, Jason Hartz, Christine Terranova, Candace Rossetti, Lisa Robinson, Billy Kelly, Jim Loughery, Heath Mink, Jimmy Hirbour, Roberta Miranda, Donna and Remco Terwal, Tarek Saba, Patricia Fabian, Steve Goldberg, Manny Connerney, Neil McPhee, Craig Herndon, Matthew Calver, Nannette Daley, Diane Hennessy, the Skoler Family, the Stern Family, the Pearlstein Family, Peter and Sharon Kline, Sokolove Law, the Dennis Family, David Bach, Ric Edelman, Ed Connarchy, Napoleon Hill, Norman Vincent Peale, Harvey Mackay, Stacy and Euell Dejesus, Nancy Doucette, the Diclemente Family, Susan and Michael Aaron, John Luther Makowiecki, Peter Cohen, Mary Gillach, Marie Presti, Ryan Persac, Jesse Gustufson, Patrick Quelly, Robyn Olson, Tom Ward, Jeff Heighton, John Hughes, Denny Bey, Michael Breda, Michael Minicucci, Robert Meegan, Joe Capone, Stephen and June McCarthy, Michael Diranian, Nancy Monbouquette, Bob Kallagher Sr. and Bob Kallagher Jr., Joe Niego, Margaret Squair and Jeanne Sherlock, Al and Vanessa Santosuosso, Karin Emerson, Jeanette Funk, Meridith Morgan, Angela Laurecella, Erica Andrade, Nicolette, Jackal, the Cappello Family, Mark Demastro, Joe Tibiero, the Fleming Family, the Kurzman Family, the Get Fresh Crew, the Wastcoat and Dalicandro Family, Janet Edsall, Joyce Kane, Jonathan Sandler, Daryl Cohan, Mark Arslan, David Eppley, George Wood, Dan Keating, Janet Porcaro, Katie McBride, Michael Davis, Justin and Mara, Adriana Scholz, Josh Brett, Celdra Harding, Melanie Swasey, Justin Hayward, Ted Duncan, Michael Casey, Chris Watroba, Jennifer Kern, Linda Wentworth, Jon Spino, Robert Guida, Scott Wheeler, Donald Rankin, Shahan Missaghian, Lisa Dean, Randy Hall, Michelle Christian Leary, Alicia Cummings, Adam Shamus, Robin Brodsky, Heddy Feldman, Liora Nielson, and Billy (thank you for taking care of my mom), Jose Abrego, Susan Abrego, Joseph Albanese, Racheline Allen, James T. Almonte, Christina Almonte, David Altman, Steven Altman, Natalia Alvarez, Jamin Edwards, Michael A. Armstrong, Dina Armstrong, Edward Asaley, Deborah Asaley, Veronica Bache, Jonathan O. Baker, Jessica Dimock, Farshad Bakhtyari, Ralph Barile, Jillian LeBlanc, Joshua Barnhardt, Gioia Barry, Adam P. Belmonte, Michelle J. Belmonte, Patrick Belmonte, Lauren Berg, Mark Beloborodov, Joe Biggins, Elizabeth Billowitz, Stephen Snyder, Elephteria Boutalis, John Brady, Judith Brady, Richard T. Broglino, Brandon Brown, Joshua Buchman, Deborah Buchman, Christine Burke, Christopher Burke, Elisa Busa, Eric Busa, Donna Busa, Richard Busa, Sr., Diane M. Busa, James Butler, John Caddell, Michelle Caddell, Marc Canner, Brian Cappello, Thomas Carr, Marlene Carr, Dharminder Chauhan, Marc Chen, Cindy Christiansen, Penn Clarke, Nolan Condon, Tim Corbett, Minda Coyle, Michele Crissman, William Crissman, Jean Curran, Myles Curran, Mark Czerwinski, James DeCelle, Sheila DeCelle, Stacy J DeJesus, Euell A DeJesus, Claudia Dell'Anno, Steven DeStefano, Peter DiClemente, Kathy DiClemente, Susan DiClemente, Bernadette Di Re, Joseph Doherty, Kenneth M. Doyle, William Doyle, Adele M. Doyle, Laurence Ducomb, Morgan Dykstar, Kimberly Etchings, Julie Fabbrucci, Franco Fazzolari, Greg Feinberg, Erica Dour, Aidan Field, Niamh Field, Josh Field, Sandra Field, Paolo Fiorina, Scott Fitzgerald, Tara Fitzgerald, David T. Fleming, Donald F. Fleming, Matthew Fletcher, Tracy Fletcher, Hugh Flynn, Anastacia Pathiakis, Stephen Fontano, Richard Forbes, Erica Fox, Kevin Fox, Michelle Fox, Dan Freeman, Amy Freeman, Eric Freeman, Rachel Freeman, Marc Freiberger, Jeanne Freiberger, Adam Gabriel, Stacey Gabriel, Lisa Gannon, Philip Gannon, Michael Gannon, Kimberly Bellavance, David Garabedian, John Gemelli, Amy Gemelli, Cairra Germain, Justin Germain, Alex Gimenez, Richard Gimenez, Adam Goff, Jared L. Goldman, Jennifer A. Goldman, Edward Gourdeau Jr, Joanne Gourdeau, Justin Gray, Kelly-Ann Charland, Mark Gredel, Alice Gredel, Gary Greenberg, Cecile Roucher-Gudwin, James Greishaber, Gina Greishaber, Elizabeth Gresser, Benjamin Gresser, Scott Grinley, Ashley Guir, Peter Gustin, Lena Haas, Bjorn Haas, John Hagenbuch, Dana Hagenbuch, Patricia Hagerty, David Hagerty, Jason Hartz, Jessica Hartz, Martha Harvey, Mirela Havens, Joaquim Havens, Stephen Hayes, Lori Hayes, S. Craig Herndon, Catherine Herndon, Gilbert Hickman III, Michael J. Higgins, Tracy Higgins, Yedidya Hilewitz, Mindy Levine, John Holland, Michelle Holland, Christine M. Horan, Hinds Howard, Erjona Howard, Frank Huckabone, Anthony Ishak, Miriam Jaffe, Martin Browne, Thomas Jasset, James Jenkins, Elizabeth Carroll, David R Jones, Judith A Jones, Catherine Jurczyk, Janet Platt, Boris Katsevman, Anna Katsevman, Scott Katz, Richard Kaufman, Stephanie Kaufman, Unsal Kaya, Heather Kearney, John Parkin Ridill, James Keck, Kelli Keck, Brian Keefe, Danielle O'Rourke, William T. Keefe, Jennifer A. Keefe, Jon D. Kelley, Rachel M. Kelley, Jeffrey Kopf, Stephanie Cogen, Michael Krause-Grosman, Ellen Krause-Grosman, Alon Landa, Ambreen Landa, Joseph Lang, Laurie Lasky, Eddie Lavalle, Michael Lavoie, Jennifer Lavoie, Julie Law, Johnathan Law, Scott Lennon, Jamie Leone, Joshua Lerman, Katrin Lerman, Keith Levine, Jodi Levine, Amir Lewkowicz, Sigal Lewkowicz, Fredric Lipsius, Setsuko Lipsius, Mike Lopez, Carol Louik, James Luciani, Joan Luciani, Mary Katherine Maco, Jonathan Madsen, Ashley Maiorano, Jaclyn Maiorano, Gene Malkin, Julia Malkin, Mark Malkin, Lillian Malkin, Matthew Malone, Dana Malone, Venugopal Mandulapalli, Aruna Panchagnula, Stephen Marchlik, Erica Marchlik, Christopher Matthews, Christine Matthews, Deborah Maw, Eric Maw, Judy McGuire, Diana McKearney, David Spezzano, Kimberly McMackin, Gina A. Medaglia, Fausto Menard, Viktoriya Bronshteyn, Adrian Mendoza, Senofer Stead, Matthew Middleton, Jennifer Middleton, Barry A. Miller, Lea A. Miller, Silva Misho, Mark Barrasso, Nitin Mittal, Fang Liu, Gavin Miyasato, Jessica Miyasato, Diane Moore, Judith Eissenberg, Jim Morando, Linda Morando, Patrick Morrissey, Sheron Morrissey, Mary Murray, Peter Murray, Shaheer Mustafa, Yolanda Coentro, Jason Myatt, Kim Myatt, Eric Navales, Emma Navales, Travis Nevers, John Newman, Peggy Newman, John Nicholas, Ursula Nicholas, James Nolan, Colette Nolan, Dana Oakes, Paula Oakes, Sean O'Brien, Jennifer O'Connell, James O'Connell, Jonathan Panush, Cristina Panza, Constance A Parish, David M. Pearlstein, Russell Perry, Emily Perry, Greg Perullo, Adriana Perullo, Melissa Pink, Nicholas Colavito, Darren Platt, Janet Porcaro, Michele Pytko, Heather Manning, Douglas Quinn, Janet Quinn, Jamie Ramola, Christian Samatis, David J Ratner, Diane J Ratner, Jeffrey Rausch, Theodore Rein, Ian Resnick, Marissa Staples, Jude Reveley, John Richardson, Lisa Richardson, Ronald Richardson, Daniel Risotti, James Risotti, William Rivell, Ian Roffman, Dennis Rohanna, Mark Rondeau, Stephanie Rondeau, Tarek Saba, Maria Patricia Fabian, Michael Sacco, Philip Sacco, Jonathan Sage, Pamela Sage, John Salo, Kristine Salo, Erik Santucci, Lisa Kepnes, Steven Santucci, Umberto Santucci, Loretta Santucci, Albert Saville, Cameron Goebeler, Farahdokht Sayan, Joan Scannell, Mark Schluntz, Tracy Heighton, Monica Shea, Joseph Shea, Sarah Sherman-Stokes, Christopher Richards, Hallie Silva, Michael J Skoler, Jennifer G Skoler, Peter Smulowitz, John Sostillio, Kevin Spezzano, Carol Spezzano, Anna Spivak, Alexander Spivak, Nicholas Stefiuk, Kristen Stefiuk, Marc J. Stern, Melissa Stern, Duncan L. Stewart, Kara M. Stewart, Marianna Iankova, Sara Swett, Kerri Zizzo,

Simon Talbot, Shervin Talebi-nejad, Michael Tashjian, Alexander Tatosky, Donna Tatosky, Margaret Tatosky, Remco Terwal, Donna Medaglia, Jordan Tishler, Lori Tishler, Jeffrey Toig, Michael Tolan, Yevgenia Khodor Tolan, Ronald Tolin, Barsha Tolin, Barbara Tornow, James Trudo, Jennifer Trudo, Richard Trunfio, Jennifer Trunfio, Mona Tse, Christina Van Dyke, Christopher Van Dyke, Cora Vestal, Hal O'Kelly Leiper, Nido Villanueva, Vicky Villanueva, Joan Vodoklys, Michael Vodoklys, Jonathan Wallach, Christine Lea Wallach, Michelle Roberts Walsh, Steven Webler, Martha Huntley, Colin Weeks, Maritza Weeks, Jodi Weiner, Anthony P. Weiss, Iris A. McNulty, Paul J. Wiley, Ellen Wing, John Wing, Sarah Witkowski, Daniel Tugender, Timothy Wolsonovich, Caren Whittington, Andrew Wylie, Alison McVie-Wylie, Stephen Yerardi, Maureen Yerardi, Peter Zaval, Jessica Zaval, Chunyu Zheng, Jie Wei, Hettie Feldman, Sam Ioannidis, Josh Ribner, Josh Ribner, Jonathan Norris, Daryl Cohan, Bud Schram, Christopher Watroba, David Yousefzadeh, Judy Moses, Kim Sullivan, Michelle Leary, Diane Carmichael, Julie Rivers, Stephen Goldberg, Mark Stiles, Laurie Ufland, Richard Vetstein, Deborah Dempsey, Mary Balsas, Mark Baxter, Jamie Baxter, Cameron B. Berkman, Eric T. Berkman, Christopher J. Bolton, Yusaku Takase, Peter Boriskin, Rachel Gans, Amy Dirazonian, Brad Hartz, Naama Hartz, Nik Ligris, Margaret L. Squair, Jeanne Sherlock, Valerie Wastcoat, John Wastcoat, Matthew Watkins, Catherine Watkins, Harvey Bravman, Scott Wheeler, Jon Sudkin, Timothy Carson, William George, Mark Arslan, Bill Brady, Julie Brady, Donald Rankin, Shahan Missaghian, Jonathan Sandler, Justin Berke, Michael Crotty, Julie Crotty, Justin Hayward, Michael Moran, Al Santosuosso, Robert B Trudo, Joseph Barka, Lisa Dean, Lisa Dean, Konstantinos Ligris, Tammy Macherides, Michelle Mazzella, Michael Casey, Randy Hall, Ryan Persac, Chuck Silverston, Josh Brett, Jon Ufland, George Wood, Katie McBride, Adriana Scholz, Arthur Deych, John Spino, Deborah Riley, Jason Luck, Linda Wentworth, Joyce Kane, Christopher Antonellis, Mary Antonellis, James A Bakum, Gioia C Perugini, Joseph Blanchard, Megan Blanchard, Jennifer J. Blum, Ellen Brakey, Hui Ying Chin, Timothy Crain, Paul DeMaio, Betty DeMaio, Jason DeMarzo, Christopher P. DiClemente, Elaine M. DiClemente, John Essery, Donna Essery, Faraz Firoozabadi, Farnaz Haghseta, Todd Foley, Melissa Foley, Matthew Forbes, Mingkun Fu, Zhen Huang, Michael Ganann, Michelle Ganann, Sonal Gandhi, John Gardiner, Joe Giantonio, Tara Gollinger, Eric Gollinger, Roberta Gordon, Jon Gordon, Eileen Haflich, Reid Haflich, Jeffrey Hannon, Jeff Heighton, Maureen Higgins, Peter J. Krug, Amanda T. Krug, Andrew H. Lee, Travinia Lee, Cathie Longo, Frederick Lopez, Amy Meeker, Jeffrey Mello, Geoffrey Meltzner, Jennifer Friedberg, Andrea Murphy, Kristin Nichols, Christopher Nichols, Deborah Oshry, Stephen Relyea, Kristin Relyea, Rhonda Rider, Marc Rosenbaum, Kathryn Rosenbaum, Kimberly Rowell, Timothy Rowell, Shannon Royer, Asri Onur Sergici, Sanem Ilgin Sergici, Jeanette Thomson, William Toll, Amber Toll, Pasquale Torcasio, Sharon Torcasio, Selim Unlu, Francisco Vega Torres, Karen Wallace, Tracy Wise Weinman, Marjorie Whittaker, Russell Whittaker, Peter Wilner, David Wilner, Cheng-Zhong Zhang, Bruce Patz, Megan Kopman, Neil Cohen, Tony Kotopoulos, Collette Brown, Kim Brady, Aaron Cohen, Crissy Lynn, Kim McAtee, Sara Rosenfeld, Samuel Webb, Chris Fleser, Margherita Ciampa-Coyne, Andrew Kadets, Joel Kinney, Robert Guida, Cynthia Lanciloti, Tiziano Doto, David Trainello, Scott Kriss, George Hailer, Elizabeth Grimes, Cyndy Forbes, Tony Tyan, Jonathan Haddad, Andria Dolce, Judy Mendel, Eric Abenaim, Phillip Koeber, Connie Radlof, Scott Goldsmith, Stacey Steck, Ted Ufland, Cedra Allen-Harding, David Eppley, Bob Benson, Seth Dailey, Alyse Dailey, Debbie Brosseau, Ed Daniels, David Shallow, Doug Crowley, Bryan Arakelian, Amber Cadorette, Carol McDonald, Maureen Mulrooney, Garret Roberts, Daniel Cosgrove, Robert Migliorini, Scott Graves, Rob Commodari, Karl Cyr, David Rich, Derek Mohamed, Peter Clay, Joseph Lagomarcino, Anne Hollows

Bibliography

Bach, David. *The Automatic Millionaire*. New York: Broadway Books, 2004.

Chilton, David Barr. *The Wealthy Barber*. New York: Three Rivers Press, 1998.

de Roos, Dolph. *Real Estate Riches*. New York: Warner, 2001.

Duncan, Todd. *High Trust Selling*. Nashville: Thomas Nelson, 2002.

Edelman, Ric. *The Truth About Money*. 3rd ed. New York: Harper Collins Publishers, 2003.

Gerber, Michael. *The E-Myth Revisited*. New York: HarperCollins Publishers, 1995.

Kiyosaki, Robert, Sharon L. Lechter. *Rich Dad Poor Dad*. New York: Hachette Book Group USA, 1997.

Mortgage Coach <www.mortgagecoach.com>

Mortgage Market Guide <www.mortgagemarketguide.com>

Loan Toolbox <www.loantoolbox.com>

Buffini and Company <www.brianbuffini.com>
> *Used by permission Buffini & Company.*
> *www.buffiniandcompany.com*

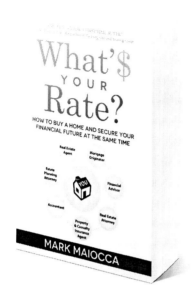

How can you use this book?

MOTIVATE

EDUCATE

THANK

INSPIRE

PROMOTE

CONNECT

Why have a custom version of *What's Your Rate?*

- Build personal bonds with customers, prospects, employees, donors, and key constituencies
- Develop a long-lasting reminder of your event, milestone, or celebration
- Provide a keepsake that inspires change in behavior and change in lives
- Deliver the ultimate "thank you" gift that remains on coffee tables and bookshelves
- Generate the "wow" factor

Books are thoughtful gifts that provide a genuine sentiment that other promotional items cannot express. They promote employee discussions and interaction, reinforce an event's meaning or location, and they make a lasting impression. Use your book to say "Thank You" and show people that you care.

CPSIA information can be obtained at www.ICGtesting.com
Printed in the USA
BVOW011819070213

312666BV00010BA/445/P

9 781599 323411